Thank you for your interest in this book. I pray that it is a help to you and an encouragement for you in your walk with the lord.

Peace be with you,

Bruce Heinly

The Minister's Pen

The Lyrics of Life and Faith

---

by

Bruce Heinly

DEDICATION

This book is dedicated to all who seek the deeper things of God. May it inspire you do just that!

Contents

CHAPTER 1: PROPHESY 10

    AND THE ANGEL SAID 11

    ENTIRE DESIRE 15

    EVERLASTING COVENANT 17

    GOD WITH US 18

    HAVE YOU SEEN JESUS 21

    IN THE CENTER OF FOREVER 25

    JESUS, OUR MESSIAH 28

    SUCH A TERRIBLE DAY 31

    THE DAY MY EYES WERE OPENED 35

    THE PROMISE OF HEAVEN 39

    THE WALLS OF SALVATION 42

    THIS MAN 44

    UNTO US 48

    WORD 52

CHAPTER 2: EVANGELISM 54

    ALL ABOUT THE BOX 55

    BETTER TO KNOW JESUS 58

    DIRTY WORN-OUT PAGES 60

    HE TOOK MY PLACE ON THE CROSS 63

    LOST AND FOUND 66

    PURE RIVER REVIVAL 70

    SEND ME 73

    SERVANT OF GOD 74

    THE REASON 78

THERE'S A GATE.. 80

TURN 'EM LOOSE, BRUCE... 82

YOU SAY COME.. 85

YOUR VERY OWN HALLELUJAH 87

CHAPTER 3: THANKSGIVING & PRAYER.............................. 89

I DON'T GOT TO BUT I GET TO 90

I NEED YOU, JESUS... 93

I TURN TO YOU... 96

IF EVER I NEEDED YOU 98

MORE THAN I DESERVE 100

MY OLD FRIEND 103

ONLY JESUS... 106

ONLY ONE 109

PARDON ME 112

PLEASE HEAR ME AS I PRAY.. 115

PRAY... 119

PRODIGAL'S LAMENT 121

SEND YOUR ANGELS... 123

THANK YOU MY FRIEND.. 125

THANKS TO YOU 127

THIS IS MY HOLY PLACE 131

UNTIL JESUS CAME INTO MY LIFE 133

YOU WITH ME... 135

YOU'RE EVERYTHING TO ME.. 137

CHAPTER 4: WISDOM 139

BE STILL.. 140

EVERY TIME I TURN AROUND 142

FORTY YEARS BEHIND, RIGHT ON TIME............................. 145

IF GOD WAS FAIR.. 147

I'M CALLED TO REACH THE GOAL 151

I'M MOVING ON... 154

IN JESUS' NAME 156

JESUS IS THE REASON 158

JUST ADD WATER.. 160

NO LOOKING BACK... 164

PEACE, BE STILL, AND KNOW 166

PEOPLE CHANGE BUT GOD STAYS THE SAME 168

PURE RELIGION 171

SIMPLY ANOINTED 173

SOMETIMES THE SCARS DON'T GO AWAY 176

WHENEVER I PULL A JONAH I GET A WHALE..................... 179

WHO IS THIS MAN 181

CHAPTER 5: IN MEMORIAM 183

AT THE GATES OF HEAVEN 184

FOREVER 187

I FOUND MYSELF IN GLORY... 189

I'LL BE LEAVING HERE WALKING IN THE LIGHT 191

I'LL SEE YOU IN HEAVEN 193

IN DUE TIME 195

NOW AND FOREVER 197

SURPRISED BY JOY.. 199

TIL YOU CAME KNOCKING 201

WELCOME HOME 203

WHEN THE CALL CAME IN 205

CHAPTER 6: PRAISE... 207

CASTING ALL MY CARES UPON YOU 208

GIVE HIM ALL THE GLORY 209

HANDS THAT NEVER FAIL.. 210

HIS PRAISE ENDURES FOREVER 212

I HAVE A REASON TO REJOICE.. 213

I WANT TO PRAISE HIM 215

IT'S NICE TO GET UP IN THE MORNING 217

LET GOD ARISE 220

LIFE STARTS NOW 221

PRAISE YE THE LORD 223

SINS DON'T STICK TO BLOOD 224

THE GREATEST THING 227

THE VICTORY IS CHRIST IN ME 230

THERE IS A NAME 233

CHAPTER 7: WORSHIP 235

HE MADE ME HOLY 236

I FOUND MY PLACE 238

IT'S YOU... 240

JESUS, I NEED YOU.. 242

KNOWING YOU.. 244

LET ME LIVE FOR YOU 247

MY REFUGE 249

THE SOUND OF HEAVEN 251

THERE'S SOMETHING IN THE AIR 253

THIS HOLY PLACE 255

TIME SPENT... 256

UNTIL I'VE GOT NOTHING LEFT 258

WORSHIP SONG 261

YOU ARE HOLY 263

YOU ARE MY LORD 264

YOU HAVE MY HEART.. 268

CHAPTER 8: FAITH 270

ABSOLUTELY FAITHFUL... 271

COMIN' ON STRONG 274

GOTTA REASON TO BELIEVE.. 275

I FEEL THE POWER 277

I'M GIVIN' IT UP.. 279

IN THE DAY OF TROUBLE 282

IN THE SPIRIT.. 284

JUST ONE THING.. 286

JUST WANT TO SEE... 288

LIVING BY FAITH 291

LIVING FOR JESUS.. 293

MORE THAN ENOUGH 295

MY DEAREST COUNTRY.. 298

ONE NATION UNDER GOD 301

POWER WALKING 303

ROLL THAT STONE AWAY.. 306

SON OF GOD 310

TIME TO GET UP 312

WE'VE GOT THE DEVIL ON THE RUN.................................. 315

WHEN WE SING HALLELUJAH 317

CHAPTER 9: HOPE 320

AS THE ROCKS BEGIN TO FLY.. 321

CAN'T STOP THE TEARS 323

ETERNITY 327

EXCEPT FOR YOU 329

FREE TO SERVE 332

HELP ME JESUS 335

HOW DO I KNOW 337

I'M A CHILD OF THE KING 342

IT WILL BE ALL RIGHT... 344

I'VE GOT JESUS HERE WITH ME 347

JUST TO SURVIVE... 349

LET NOT YOUR HEART BE TROUBLED 352

ONE HOPE 353

ONE STEP BELOW THE BOTTOM 355

PUT IT IN THE HANDS OF GOD... 358

YOU SPEAK THE TRUTH... 360

CHAPTER 10: LOVE.. 365

A LOVE LIKE THIS.. 366

BEAUTIFUL BRIDE.. 368

BEYOND THE CROSS 370

CAPTURED BY THE LOVE 372

COVER ME (MY FATHER'S CHILD)................................... 374

FAITH, HOPE, AND LOVE.. 376

FALL IN LOVE WITH YOU.. 379

GOD'S LIKE THAT 380

GOD'S LOVE 383

GOOD, GOOD FRIDAY 385

IT'S A SPIRITUAL THING.. 387

LOVE FINDS A WAY.. 390

MERCY WAS WAITING THERE FOR ME 392

OH, WHAT LOVE.. 394

ONE THING... 395

ORIGINAL GRACE 397

YOU MUST HAVE LOVED ME... 402

CHAPTER 1: PROPHESY

1

AND THE ANGEL SAID

She Was Getting On In Years

Unable To Have A Child

Elizabeth Was Righteous Before God

Her Husband Was A Priest

And His Prayers For A Son

Were On His Mind

As He Entered The Holy Place

And The Angel Said

Zechariah, Don't Be Afraid

God Has Heard Your Prayer

Elizabeth Will Have A Son Named John

There Will Be Joy And Gladness

And Rejoicing At His Birth

He Will Turn The Hearts Of Many

To The Lord

After Six Months Had Gone By

The Angel Was Sent Again

This Time To A Young Girl Named Mary

A Virgin Betrothed To Joseph

Who Was A Man Of The House Of David

And Everything They Knew

Was About To Change, And The Angel Said

Greetings, Oh Favored One

The Lord Is With You

But This Troubled Her

And She Didn't Know What To Do

Mary, Don't Be Afraid

For You Have Found Great Favor With God

And Behold, You Shall Conceive

And Bear A Son, And The Angel Said

You Will Give Him The Name Of Jesus

The Son Of The Most High God

He Shall Be Great,

And His Kingdom Shall Never End

Overshadowed Now With Power

The Holy Spirit Is With You

And This Child Shall Be Born

The Son Of God

And Mary Said

My Soul Magnifies The Lord

And My Spirit Rejoices In My Savior

For Behold, From Now On

Generations Shall Call Me Blessed

For He, The Mighty One

Has Done Great Things

So In A Stable He Was Born

In A Manger He Was Laid

Such A Humble Start

For The Mighty Son Of God

And As The Shepherds

Watched Their Flocks That Night

An Angel Came To Them

And In The Glory Of The Lord

They Were Afraid

And The Angel Said

Fear Not, For Behold

I Bring Glad Tidings Of Great Joy

For Unto You, This Day

The Savior Is Born

Glory To God In The Highest

And On Earth There Shall Be Peace

Peace Among Those

With Whom He Is Pleased

And The Shepherds Said

Let Us All Now Walk The Path

That Leads To The Holy One

Jesus, Our Messiah, Has Come

Amen! Today Our Eyes Shall See

The Gift For All Humanity

From God . . . To Man . . . His Son\\

ENTIRE DESIRE

By The Power Of Your Word

Through The Message I Have Heard

In The Passion Of The Cross

The Salvation Of The Lost

In The Healing Of The Sick

The Renewing Of The Mind

The Deaf Can Hear, The Blind Can See

And I Have Come To Find

Your Entire Desire Is Revealed

And I'm Humbled By Your Mercy

And Your Grace

And I'm Broken By Your Presence

In This Place

You Have Given Me All I Need To See

That You Want To Be Here With Me

And I Bow Before You Now Almighty God

I'm Not Worthy Of This Honor You Bestow

Yet, You Lift Me Up With Love

And Give Me Hope

And By Your Holy Spirit, This I Know

Your Entire Desire Is Revealed

When I Wake Up In The Morning

When I Go To Sleep At Night

Through The Good Times

And The Hard Times

With You It Comes Out Right

You Have Given Me All I Need To See

That You Want To Be Here With Me\\

EVERLASTING COVENANT

Take This Bread, Take And Eat

This Is My Body Broken For You

I Am The Bread Of Life

The One And Only Sacrifice

Worthy Of The Cross

Take This Cup, Take And Drink

This Is My Blood Shed For You

Everlasting Covenant, Poured Out For You

For The Forgiveness Of Sins

And Remember This

Whenever You Do This

Do This In Remembrance Of Me

GOD WITH US

Many A Day That I Have Spent

Wondering Why The Father Sent

His Only Son To Be Born As One Of Us

God With Us

Wonderful Counselor, Jesus, My Lord

The Prophets Have Spoken

The Time Had Come

The Angels Proclaimed

A Child Is Born Unto Us

God With Us

Destined To Die For All Mankind

Despised And Rejected

He Laid Down His Life

This Child Who Took His Place

On The Cross For Us

God With Us

God So Loved The World

He Gave His Only Son

That Whoever Believes

Would Not Perish

But Have Eternal Life

God With Us

God So Loved The World

He Sent His Only Son

Not To Condemn The World

But To Save Them From Their Sins

God With Us

Destined To Die For All Mankind

Despised And Rejected

He Laid Down His Life

This Child Who Took His Place

On The Cross For Us

God With Us

God With Us, God With Us

Emanuel, The King Of Kings

Jesus Christ

God With Us

God With Us, The Holy One

The Son Of God And The Son Of Man

The Way, The Truth And The Life

Given To Us

God With Us\\

HAVE YOU SEEN JESUS

Used To Live Outside Jerusalem

Back In The Day

Heard About The Son Of God

The Miracles

And The Things He Had To Say

Heard He Was Coming To Jerusalem

So I Set Out On My Way

But On The Way I Heard

Of Trouble In The Land

I Didn't Understand, I Didn't Understand

How Could They Do Those Things

To Such A Man As This

I Can't Believe These Things I've Heard

Don't They Know This Man Is Jesus

The Christ

And His Presence Here Is Fulfillment

Of The Word?

I Must Hurry Now And Make My Way

Make My Way Into The Town

I Need To Know If I'm Too Late

Still, I Must Find Him If He Can Be Found

Have You Seen Jesus?

I Heard They've Taken Him Away

I'm Afraid That I Won't Find Him Today

Have You Seen Jesus?

They Say He's Gone And All Is Lost

I Heard They Made Him Carry

His Own Cross

Have You Seen Jesus?

He Was Battered, He Was Beaten

He Was Torn

My King Wears A Crown Of Thorns

Have You Seen Jesus?

They Tell Me He Is Gone

But He's Done Nothing Wrong

What's This I See At The Temple Of God

The Curtain Is Torn, It's Torn In Two

This Is The End, The End Of This Age

And The Beginning Of Something New

And I Believe The Stories Are True

And Just As He Said, Jesus Will Rise Again

And I Will Wait In This Place

For Three Days More, I Shall Stay

And I Will Fast, And I Will Pray

Just To See Him

To See Him Face To Face

Have You Seen Jesus

He's No Longer In The Grave

The Stone's Been Rolled Away

Have You Seen Jesus?

Do You Remember What He Said?

He Has Risen From The Dead

Have You Seen Jesus?

He Is The Lord, Our God And King

He Shed His Blood For Our Sins

He's Alive, He Is With Us Here, Today

Turn To Him And Pray

What Kind Of Love Is This I See

A Love That Would Die To Set Me Free

What Kind Of Friend

Would Lay Down His Life

And Go To The Cross As My Sacrifice

Lord, Your Love, Your Love For Me

Is All That I Desire\\

IN THE CENTER OF FOREVER

From Point To Point, The Line Was Drawn

In The Center Of Forever

God Decided Then That There Was Time

Created In His Image

In The Center Of Forever

We Live And Breathe And Move

To Walk The Line

In The Center Of Forever

It's Where I Need To Stay

In The Center Of His Love And Grace

And Mercy Everyday

Jesus Is The Answer To Every Prayer I Pray

In The Center Of Forever

On The Straight And Narrow Way

As Time Goes By, On Down The Line

God Is Good All The Time

Leading All Believers Day To Day

Don't You Worry About Tomorrow

At The End There Is No Sorrow

Jesus On The Line, He Is The Way

On The Level, On The Line

Jesus Knew When It Was Time

To Pay Up On The Cross For All Our Sins

In The Center Of Forever

He Rose Up From The Dead

And In The Spirit

We Can All Be Born Again

In The Center Of Forever

It's Where I Need To Stay,

In The Center Of His Love And Grace

And Mercy Everyday

Jesus Is The Answer To Every Prayer I Pray

In The Center Of Forever

On The Straight And Narrow Way

He's The Alpha And Omega

The Beginning And The End

Jesus Went To Heaven

But He's Coming Back Again

In The Center Of Forever

In The Spirit, We Abide

And At The End Of The Line, We Go On\\

JESUS, OUR MESSIAH

Once Again We Gather Here

To Celebrate The Birthday

Of Our Savior, Our Messiah

Once Again We Hear The Words

The Story Of A Savior

Born In Bethlehem, Our Messiah

Once Again We Bring Our Gifts

To Celebrate The Greatest Gift

Of Jesus, Our Messiah

Once Again We Gather Here

To Lift Our Hands

And Bless The Name Of Jesus

Our Messiah

Once Again We Turn Our Hearts

To See The Son Of God

Who Came To Save Us, Holy Jesus

Once Again, Inviting All

To Join Us In A Christmas Feast

For Jesus, Our Messiah

Once Again We Gather Here

Remembering And Worshiping

Our Savior, Our Messiah

Once Again We Look Upon

This Baby In The Manger

And We Sing To Him

Our Messiah

Once Again We Sing Our Songs

Of Christmas As We Think About

Our Savior, Our Messiah

Once Again We Gather Here

To Open Up Our Hearts And Souls

To Jesus, Our Messiah

Once Again We Gather Here

To Celebrate The Birthday Of Our Savior

Holy Jesus

Once Again The Music Plays

And Trumpets Sound

To Praise The Name

Of Jesus,, Our Messiah

For Unto Us This Child Was Born

Unto Us The Son Was Given

And The Government Shall Be

Upon His Shoulders

Wonderful, Counselor

Everlasting Father

The Mighty God

And The Prince Of Peace\\

SUCH A TERRIBLE DAY

She Wasn't Around

When The Word Came Down

Don't Eat From That Tree

And Even Though Adam Knew The Truth

Eve Ate, And He Agreed

Surely, We Won't Die, She Said

This Fruit Looks Good To Eat

The Serpent Had Timed It Perfectly

God's Man Had Been Deceived

Such A Terrible Day

Such A Terrible Day That Would Be

When Man Decided He Was King

Of His Own Destiny

Such A Terrible Day, The End Of An Age

Where Man And God Had Fellowship

And Man Turned Away

The Rain Came Down For Forty Days

And The Ark Was Riding High

Noah And His Family

Were The Only To Survive

And When It Had Subsided

They Stepped Out On The Land

And God Said He Would Never Do

Anything Like This Again

Such A Terrible Day

Such A Terrible Day That Would Be

When Man Decided He Was King

Of His Own Destiny

Such A Terrible Day, The End Of An Age

Where Man And God Had Fellowship

And Man Turned Away

The Blood Ran Down Upon His Face

From The Crown They Made Of Thorns

The Pain That Nailed Him To The Cross

Matched Only By The Scorn

He Did Not Come To Judge

But As The Sacrificial Lamb

But The Son Of God Was Judged There

For The Sins Of Every Man

Such A Terrible Day

Such A Terrible Day That Would Be

When Man Decided He Was King

Of His Own Destiny

Such A Terrible Day, The End Of An Age

Where Man And God Had Fellowship

And Man Turned Away

The Work Is Done, The Plan Complete

And Jesus Is Alive

He Rose Up From The Grave, A King

And Ascended To The Sky

He'll Come Again And In The End

A Judgment Day Awaits

Will You Believe Him Now

Or Will It Be Too Late

Such A Terrible Day

Such A Terrible Day That Would Be

When Man Decided He Was King

Of His Own Destiny

Such A Terrible Day, The End Of An Age

Where Man And God Had Fellowship

And Man Turned Away\\

THE DAY MY EYES WERE OPENED

He Stood Right There

Before Me

It's A Day I'll Never Forget

He Was Wearing A Robe

With A Sash Of Gold

There Across His Chest

His Head And His Hair

Were White Like Wool

And His Eyes

Like Fiery Flames

His Feet Were As Bright

As Bronze Refined

And His Voice

Was Like Thundering Waves

I Knew That He Had Risen

I Saw The Tomb

Now Empty

Where He Was Laid

But When I Saw Him Then

I Fell As One Dead

And He Said

Don't Be Afraid

I Am The First

I Am The Last

I Am The Living One Who Died

But Look, I'm Alive!

I Hold The Keys Of Death

And The Grave

I Am The One You Can Turn To

And Be Saved

The Days That I Remember

Before I Met My Savior

Are The Days

That I Could Just As Soon Forget

Because The Love I Found In Jesus

Has Changed My Life Forever

No Looking Back, No Doubt

No Regrets

The Day My Eyes Were Opened

I Felt The Arms Of Satan

Open Up

And Let Me Go

The Day My Eyes Were Opened

I Felt The Love Of Jesus

Change Me

Change Me

And Make Me Whole

There's A Power In This Place

It's Jesus And His Amazing Grace

He Was Crucified And Died

But He Rose Again

Yes, That's Right

He Took Your Place

Yes, There's A Power

In This Place

It's The Power

Of Gods Saving Grace

Call On Jesus

Your Life Will Change

The Holy Ghost Is Here

And He Knows Your Name\\

THE PROMISE OF HEAVEN

Bright Lights Flashing In The Sky

So Beautiful, So Colorful

Someone Hanging On A Cross

Reaching Out To Me

Wholeheartedly

And The Table Is Set

With A Feast For A King

The Light Of The World

Covers Everything

Oh, Yes, This Must Be Heaven

Just Look At These Streets Of Gold

And The Mansions Stand So Proud

On This Walkway In The Clouds

I Must Be In Heaven

I Can't Describe How It Feels

To Know That He Is Here With Me

The Son Of God, The Holy One

The King Of Kings

The Savior Of The World

The Promise Of Heaven

When I Wake Up From This Dream

So Beautiful, So Colorful

I Will Know Just What It Means

Reaching Out To Me, Wholeheartedly

My Mind Is Set On The King Of Kings

The Light Of The World

Covers Everything

Oh, Yes, I'll Be In Heaven

I'll See The Streets Of Gold

Where The Mansions Stand So Proud

On This Walkway In The Clouds

I'll Be In Heaven

I Can't Describe How It Feels

To Know That He Is Here With Me

The Son Of God, The Holy One

The King Of Kings

The Savior Of The World

The Promise Of Heaven

Bright Lights Flashing In The Sky

So Beautiful, So Colorful

Someone Hanging On A Cross

Reaching Out To Me

Wholeheartedly

Changed In The Twinkling

Of An Eye

When Jesus Comes For You And I

Watch The Sky

For The Promise Of Heaven

The Promise Of Heaven\\

THE WALLS OF SALVATION

The Walls Of Salvation Surround This City

Open The Gates

That The Righteous Nation May Enter In

The Walls Of Salvation Surround This City

Without Compromise

By Faith, You Can Enter In

In The Name Of Jesus

The Creator Of All Things

Peace Has Been Established

And In Us, The Work Is Done

In The Name Of Jesus

The Author And Finisher Of Our Faith

Salvation Will Be The Song That We Sing

And Our Song Of Salvation In The City

Will Be Heard Throughout The Nations

Proclaiming The Name Above All Names

This Song Of Salvation

Is The Song I Forever Shall Sing

The Desire Of My Soul

Is For His Name

In The Walls Of Salvation

We Can Have Perfect Peace

If Our Mind Is Stayed On Him

The King Of Kings

In The Walls Of Salvation

The Lord Is Our Everlasting Rock

And The Way Of The Righteous

Is Level And Straight

The Walls Of Salvation Surround This City

Open The Gates

That The Righteous Nation May Enter In

The Walls Of Salvation Surround This City

Without Compromise

By Faith, You Can Enter In\\

THIS MAN

(The Gospel According To Thomas)

This Man, This Man

Saw Deep Into My Soul

This Man Said, Follow Me

I Said, Yes, Yes I Will Go

This Man, Like No Other Man

Touched The Lame

And Made Them Whole

This Man Fed Five Thousand

With Two Fish And Five Small Loaves

This Man, This Man

Healed The Sick And Raised The Dead

This Man, Spoke With Power

And We Heard Every Word He Said

This Man Was Teaching

Of A Kingdom To Come

Where God Is Our Father

And Jesus, His Son

But This Man Was Hated

For Speaking The Truth

This Man Was Chastised For Love

This Man Was Taken

By Those He Came To Know

This Man Was Betrayed With A Kiss

This Man, They Said, Had To Go

This Man Was Whipped

And Beaten With Fists

This Man Was Mocked

He Was Spit On And Kicked

This Man Was Brought

To The Judge To Be Tried

They Wanted Him Crucified

This Man, This Man

Was Despised And Rejected Of Men

This Man, Was Wounded

He Was Bruised For All Of Our Sins

This Man Who Did No Wrong

Was Nailed To A Cross

And Sentenced To Die

This Man, Before

He Drew His Last Breath

Said Forgive Them

For They Don't Know Why

This Man Was Placed In A Tomb

Sealed By The Guards With A Stone

But This Man, After Three Days Dead

Came And Found Us At Home

He Said Touch My Hands

Put Your Hand On My Side

I Want You To See That I Am Alive

My Lord And My God

Are The Words That I Cried

As I Fell Down And Worshipped This Man

This Man Said Now

You Can Come To The Father

Ask Anything In My Name

This Man Said Go

You Can Do Greater Things

Your Life Will Not Be The Same

This Man Is Jesus, God In The Flesh

This Man Has Saved Us

From The Power Of Death

This Man Has Given Us Life Forevermore

This Man Is Jesus, My Lord\\

UNTO US

Can't Believe This Good News

I Have Heard Today, This Wonderful Day

Found Out God So Loved The World

He Gave His Son, Our Souls To Save

Found Out That Our Savior Came

From Heaven For The Lost

Found Out That He Took Our Place

And Died Upon The Cross

Found Out We Don't Have To

Be Afraid Anymore

Because I Heard The Angel Did Say

Unto Us A Child Is Born

This Day, This Day, This Wonderful Day

Unto Us A Son Is Given

A Shining Light To Show The Way

Born To Die And Save Us

From The Punishment Of Sin

Born Of The Spirit

Born To Rise Again

Unto Us

Can't Believe This Good News

I Have Heard Today, This Wonderful Day

Found Out That The Love Of God

In Christ Is Here Today, To Stay

Wonderful, Counselor

The Mighty God Is He

The Everlasting Father

He Is The Prince Of Peace

And His Grace Is Sufficient

He Is Strong When We Are Weak

Because I Heard The Angel Did Say

Unto Us A Child Is Born

This Day, This Day, This Wonderful Day

Unto Us A Son Is Given

A Shining Light To Show The Way

Born To Die And Save Us

From The Punishment Of Sin

Born Of The Spirit

Born To Rise Again

Unto Us

Can't Believe How Good It Feels

To Turn To God And Pray Today

Knowing That He Loves Me

And Will Never Turn His Face Away

Baptized In The Holy Ghost

You Know I Feel The Love

Jesus Sent His Spirit To Keep

My Mind On Things Above

And His Words Give Me Life

As I Walk In The Light

Because I Heard The Angel Did Say

Unto Us A Child Is Born

This Day, This Day, This Wonderful Day

Unto Us A Son Is Given

A Shining Light To Show The Way

Born To Die And Save Us

From The Punishment Of Sin

Born Of The Spirit

Born To Rise Again

Unto Us\\

WORD

I'm Connected To The Soul-saving

Mind-changing

Body-healing, Spirit-moving

Life-giving Word Of God

It's A Double-edged Sword

Cutting Soul And Spirit

Like An Axe Down The Middle Of A Log

It Cuts Away My Doubt

It Makes Me Feel Alive

There's Power In The Living Word

And I'm Satisfied

The Holy Ghost Is Giving Me

Assurance Of Things To Come

And I'll Run The Good Race

Until My Work On Earth Is Done

I Believe In The Word That's Alive

And Living In Me

Because The Word Found Me In Sin

And Set Me Free

Speaking What I Hear In The Word

Keeps My Soul In Line

Letting Patience Have Its Perfect Work

I'm Feeling Fine

The Word Is Searching My Heart

And Testing My Mind, As I Follow Jesus

And I Leave This World Behind

My Faith Comes By Hearing

And The Word Gives Me Ears To Hear

My Hope Is Secure

As The Coming Of Christ Draws Near

My God Is A Mighty Mountain

And His Love Is Bigger Still

And When He Asks, Will You Feed My Sheep

I Say, Yes, I Will\\

CHAPTER 2:
EVANGELISM

2

ALL ABOUT THE BOX

There Was A Feeling In The Air

That He Hadn't Felt Before

The Excitement Was Getting Stronger

He Couldn't Wait Any Longer

He Had To Know

They Gathered All The Children

And Spoke To Them Of Jesus

And The Boxes They Were Handing Out

Were Not Like Anything He'd Seen Before

Then, As He Watched Them Find

The Gifts That Were Inside

It Brought A Smile To His Face

And Something More

This Was A Feeling He'd Never Felt Before

It Was All About The Box

It Was All About The Love

It Was All About The Peace Of God

And The Hope

That They Were Bringing Now

It Was All About The Box

And The Joy That It Brought

As They Opened Up To Receive

The Love Of God

It Was All About The Box

Then He Opened Up His Box

And Those Around Him Were Surprised

Some Of The Gifts In His Box

Were For A Girl, Not For A Boy

The Tears Fell From His Eyes

But Still, He Had His Smile

As He Said, I Know That Jesus Sent Me This

I Can Finally Give My Sister A Gift

Oh, It Was All About The Box

It Was All About The Love

It Was All About The Peace Of God

And The Hope

That They Were Bringing Now

It Was All About The Box

And The Joy That It Brought

As They Opened Up To Receive

The Love Of God

It Was All About The Box

Let The Children Come

And Forbid Them Not

For Such Is The Kingdom Of Heaven

It's All About The Box\\

BETTER TO KNOW JESUS

Better To Have

Something Real In My Life

Better Than What This World Has To Give

Better To Love

Than To Know Wrong From Right

Better To Live

Better To Walk In The Light

Better To Know Jesus

As A Brother And A Friend

Better To Understand Who God Is

Better To Give Myself

To The Creator Of All Things

Better To Know Jesus, And Believe

Better For Me

To Turn To The Lord

Leave My Way Of Life

And Change My Mind

Better To Fall

On My Knees In Prayer

Better To Be Saved By Grace

Through Faith

Better To Be

Forgiven For My Sins

Crucified With Christ And Born Again

Better To See

Through Eyes Of Love

Better To Understand The Cross

Better To Know Jesus

As A Brother And A Friend

Better To Understand Who God Is

Better To Give Myself

To The Creator Of All Things

Better To Know Jesus, And Believe\\

DIRTY WORN-OUT PAGES

I'm Older Now Than I Ever Thought

That I Would Ever Be

It Makes Me Laugh

Because I Thought I Was Done

Back In Ninety-Three

Now, Many Years Later

I'm Still Living The Life

And I'm Fighting The Good Fight

It Ain't Over 'Till It's Over

And God Turns Out The Lights

These Dirty, Worn Out Pages

Of My Holy Bible

Are What Keeps Me Going Strong

And The Message You Will Find

On Those Worn-Out Pages

Is Jesus All Day Long

Truth Be Told, It Never Gets Old

It Will Be There Long After I'm Gone

So Open Up Those Dirty, Worn Out Pages

Of Your Bible And Pass That Message Along

The Dirty, Worn Out Pages Of My Holy Bible

Tell The Story Of My Life

It Was In Those Pages

That I Found The Reason

To Follow Jesus Christ

It Gives Me Joy When I Remember

The Lives That Have Been Changed

When I Opened Up The Dirty

Worn Out Pages Of My Bible

And Spoke Those Words Again

Sometimes My Hands Get Dirty In The Fields

When I'm Bringing The Harvest In

But There's Still So Many Souls Out There

That Need To Be Born Again

So, I'll Open Up Those Dirty

Worn Out Pages Of My Bible

And I'll Speak The Word That's True

Those Seeds That I Plant

Along The River Of Life

Will Come Back Bearing Fruit\\

HE TOOK MY PLACE ON THE CROSS

I've Fallen Short Of The Glory

Fallen Short Of The Glory Of God

But I Know That I Am Forgiven

Forgiven And Delivered From Sin

I Couldn't Do It

And The Same Goes For You

We're In This Together

And He'll Bring Us Through

God Is Love, And Love Paid The Cost

When He Took Our Place On The Cross

Jesus Took My Place On The Cross

Jesus Knows That Without Him, I'm Lost

And I Know That I Am

Redeemed By His Blood

The Blood Shed For Me On That Cross

Let God Be True, Without Me, Without You

In Christ Alone All Things Become New

He Said, I Have The Keys

To Death And The Grave

And I Am Alive, So Don't Be Afraid

Ask And Receive That You're Joy May Be Full

We're In This Together

And He'll Bring Us Through

God Is Love, And Love Paid The Cost

When He Took Our Place On The Cross

He Ascended To Heaven

And Sent Me His Spirit

To Be Forever With Me

And The Holy Ghost Knows

What I Need Every Day

And Leads Me Along As I Pray

And Then On That Day

When I Stand Before God

And He Looks To Jesus

Who Gives Him The Nod

I'll Fall At His Feet; My Lord And My God

He Took My Place On The Cross

Jesus Took My Place On The Cross

Jesus Knows That Without Him, I'm Lost

And I Know That I Am

Redeemed By His Blood

The Blood Shed For Me On That Cross\\

LOST AND FOUND

A Lost And Found Is What We Need

The Pastor Said To Me

When The People Leave

Their Stuff Behind

It Needs A Place To Be

A Box Or A Bin Is What Comes To Mind

Look Around As See What You Can Find

To Keep The Things

That People Leave Behind

To Keep The Things

That People Leave Behind

So I Found An Old Aquarium

In The Attic On A Shelf

I Think This Will Do Nicely

If I Do Say So Myself

Then I Made A Sign Engraved In Wood

And Glued It To The Side

Lost And Found, It Said

For The Things You Leave Behind

Lost And Found

For The Things You Leave Behind

A Pair Of Glasses, A Couple Of Books

And A Colorful Set Of Keys

Through The Glass

They Saw The Things They Lost

And Were As Happy As Could Be

Then One Day A Note Was Left

In With The Lost And Found

Please, Lord, It Said, Set Them Free

From The Chains That Have Them Bound

Set Them Free

From The Chains That Have Them Bound

As I Wiped The Teardrops From My Eyes

It Was More Than I Could Bear

I Had To Stop And Bow My Head

I Had To Make My Prayer

They Can't Make It On Their Own, Lord

They Really Need To Know

This Message Of The Cross

That We Share

Jesus Loves Them

They Need To Know He Cares

Lost And Found

Is More Than What It Seems

God Knows The Names Of Everyone

The Lost And The Redeemed

Lost And Found

Write Your Name And Toss It In

God Knows The Prayers Of All Who Call

And He'll Find You

In The Lost And Found

I Placed The Note Back In The Box

For Everyone To Read

And Within A Week

More Notes Were Added

For God To Meet Their Needs

Salvation For The Lost

And The Faith Just To Believe

All Seeking Their Redemption

All Wanting To Be Free

All Praying For The Truth

To Set Them Free\\

PURE RIVER REVIVAL

There's A Pure, Pure River

Flowing From The Throne

The Throne Of God The Father

And The Lamb

And In The Midst Of That River

With The Promise Of Forever

The Spirit Of Our Savior, Jesus Christ

Take Me Down To The River

And Wash Away My Sins

Take Me Down To The River

And Make Me Whole

Take Me Down To That Pure River

I Need To Be Born Again

Take Me Down To That River

And Free My Soul

The Lord Of The Harvest

Is Sending Out His Word

He's Sending You And Me

To Testify Of What We've Heard

Jesus Is Coming To Take His People Home

But Until Then The World Needs To Know

Send Me, Lord, To My Neighbor

Send Me, Lord, To My Friends

Send Me, Lord, To The Stranger

Who Needs To Be Born Again

Send Me, Lord, Now, Into The World

That Everyone May See

That Jesus Has Come To Set Them Free

With Signs And Wonders Show The World

There's Power In The Blood

Let Everything You Do Now

Testify Of His Great Love

God Sent His Only Son

Into The World To Save The Lost

And Jesus Took Our Sins Upon The Cross

God Is Pouring Out His Spirit

And The Way Has Been Prepared

Tell The World That Jesus Loves Them

And Show Them That You Care

'Cause If They Turn Away From Him

They'll Suffer Without End

So Tell The World

They Must Be Born Again\\

SEND ME

As I Stand Before You, Lord

Overcome By Your Love

Knowing I'm So Undeserving

Of This Mercy From Above

When You Need To Call On Me

I Shall Turn To You

Speak And I Will Hear Your Voice

Knowing Then What I Shall Do

As I Step Into The Night

Seeking To Reveal Your Light

Let My Words Be True And Right

By Your Spirit, Not By Might

With Ears To Hear The Words You Speak

With Eyes To See What Needs To Be

Walking With You In The Light

I Ask Only That Your Will Be Done In Me

Send Me\\

SERVANT OF GOD

Oh, Servant Of God

Forever Faithful To The Call

You've Learned To Do It All

Through Christ Who Strengthens You

Oh, Servant Of God

I Can See It On Your Face

The Reflection Of God's Grace

That Tells Me Who You Are

Oh, Servant Of God

I Can See It In Your Eyes

Anticipation Of The Prize

The Prize That Waits For You

Oh, Servant Of God

I Can Hear It In Your Voice

The Passion Of The Cross

That Lives In You

To The Ends Of The Earth

You Speak Of A New Birth

That Is Offered Now

To All Who Will Believe

You Speak Of Jesus Christ

The Way, The Truth, The Life

And Of A Love That Overcomes

To Meet Our Needs

You Sow The Seeds Of Faith

And Patiently You Wait

And You Hope The Day Will Come

When They Will Grow

For It's Not By Your Own Power

Or By Your Will That Things Are Done

But By The Spirit Of The Lord

The Battles Are Won

Healing Broken Hearts

Bringing Good News To The Poor

You Tell The World Of Jesus Love

And Of Life Forevermore

Laying Hands To Heal The Sick

And With A Word The Dead Are Raised

Casting Out The Evil One

By The Power Of Jesus Name

And When The Work Has All Been Done

And When The Good Race Has Been Run

And You're Standing Tall

Before The King Of Kings

He Speaks With A Great Voice

That Makes Your Heart Rejoice

You've Done Well, My Child

Now Let The Angels Sing

Oh, Servant Of God

Forever Faithful To The Call

You've Learned To Do It All

Through Christ Who Strengthens You

Oh, Servant Of God

I Can See It On Your Face

The Reflection Of God's Grace

That Tells Me Who You Are

Oh, Servant Of God

I Can See It In Your Eyes

Anticipation Of The Prize

The Prize That Waits For You

Oh, Servant Of God

I Can Hear It In Your Voice

The Passion Of The Cross

That Lives In You\\

THE REASON

If You're Trying To Figure Out

What This Life Is All About

When It Feels Like, Like You're Drowning

In The Middle, In The Middle Of A Drought

And When Nothing Makes Sense

No Place To Stop And Get Some Rest

Come To Jesus And It Will Be Alright

This Is The Reason I Do What I Do

This Is The Reason And It's All About You

This Is The Reason That I Do What I Can

Why I Give It All Away

Why I Say The Things I Say

Why I Take The Time To Help You Find

The Way, The Truth, The Life

Yes, The Reason For It All Is This

That God Exists

Maybe You're Hurting

Through And Through

I Can Tell You What I'd Like To Do

Come And Sit With Me

And Let Me Pray With You

What He Did For Me He'll Do For You

I Know That I Know It's True

Come To Jesus And It Will Be Alright

Come And Talk With Me A Little While

And Listen To The Story Of How

How My Life Has Changed

Since I Met Jesus Christ

Alive And Living In Me

I Let Him In And Now I See

My Sins Are Gone, I've Been Set Free

And Everyone Can See Jesus In Me\\

THERE'S A GATE

There's A Gate

Standing Wide Open

Big Enough For All To See

And Beyond This Gate

Is A Lake Of Fire

That Burns For Eternity

There's A Gate

Standing Wide Open

Big Enough For All To Find

And The Lake Of Fire

You Will Find Inside

Is For Satan And All Of His Kind

So Don't Enter The Gate That Is Wide

Don't Enter The First Gate You See

There's Another Gate You Can Enter

Paid For At Calvary

There's A Way You Can Take

Straight And Narrow

To The Gate

Of The Blood-bought Redeemed

Where The Way Was Paid

By The Blood Of Christ

When He Died On Calvary

There's A Gate

That Leads To A Kingdom

Where Jesus Reigns As King

And The Love Of God Is Eternal

Just Believe And Enter In\\

TURN 'EM LOOSE, BRUCE

They Came As One

All On The Run

Bound In Their Sin

They Came To Mock The Son

They Came To Watch Him

On The Cross

And His Blood Was Shed For Them

So That They Would Not Be Lost

He Said, Father, Forgive Them

They Really Do Not Know

The Desire Of His Heart

Was To Let Them Go

And Now All Who Believe

Have A Mission To Fulfill

Take The Gospel To The World

And Keep It Real

Turn 'em Loose, Bruce

Set 'em Free, Lee

Let Them Turn To The Lord

And They Will See\\

You Got To Bring 'em To The Light

And Get 'em Grounded In The Word

Then The Gospel Will Be Spread By Them

All Across The World

Tell 'em Jesus Is Alive And Well

Risen From The Dead

Call On Him, He'll Hear Your Prayer

And You'll Be Born Again

Everything You Need For Life

Is Found In Knowing Jesus Christ

The Way, The Truth, The Life

The Prince Of Peace
Say The Name

The Name Of Jesus

He Is The Son Of God

The Lamb That Was Slain

He Rose Again

Up From The Grave

And Now All Who Call Upon Him

Shall Be Saved

He Said, I Go

To Prepare A Place For You

If It Were Not So

I Would Have Let You Know

Don't Let Your Heart Be Troubled

Believe In Me

Take The Gospel To The World

And Keep It Free\\

YOU SAY COME

You Say Come, Come To The Water

You Say Come, Come And Thirst No More

You Say Come When You Are Weary

Come Unto Me, Come Unto Me

In The Water, The Living Water

We Shall Never, Never Be Alone

And One Day You'll Come Again

And Take Us Home

Lord, I Offer Up My Life To You

All My Sins To Wash Away

I Fall Down And Cry Thanksgivings Unto You

In The Wonder Of Your Mercy

And Your Grace

Only You Can Change This Heart Of Mine

Only You Can Save My Soul

Only You Know All That I Have Done

And Still, You Say Come

Nothing Compares To This Love I've Found

Living Water For My Soul

I Was So Lost But Then You Came To Me

You Found Me In My Sin

And Made Me Whole

Such Forgiveness I Have Never Known

Such Compassion Through And Through

What Kind Of Love Is This

That I Have Found

Lord Jesus, I Come To You\\

YOUR VERY OWN HALLELUJAH

Born To Die On A Cross, But Why

Because God So Loved The World

Jesus Took The Punishment

For Sin Upon Himself

This Is Why He Came

To Take Away our Sins

This Is Why He Came, It's What Jesus Did

Mankind Needed A Savior

And Jesus Is That Man

He's No Longer Dead, He Rose Again

And He's Reaching Out

So Turn To The Lord And Pray today

His Mercy Endures Forever

This Is Why He Came

To Take Away Your Sins

This Is Why He Came, It's What Jesus Did

Sing Hallelujah, with Jesus

You Can Rise Up And Live

Sing Hallelujah, He Will Do For You

What Only He Can Do

Sing Hallelujah, It's A Gift Of Love

Covered By The Blood

And This Can Be, For You, Forever

Your Very Own Hallelujah

It's What Jesus Did

You See It's All About The Love

That God Has For You

It's All About A Way For You

To Change The Things You Do

It's All About Joy And Hope

It's All About New Life

It's All About The Savior Jesus Christ

Jesus Put Your Spirit In Me

Make Me Holy, Set Me Free

I Come Before You, On My Knees

Take Me, Change Me, Fill Me, Please

Jesus, You Are All I'll Ever Need\\

CHAPTER 3:
THANKSGIVING
and PRAYER

3

I DON'T GOT TO BUT I GET TO

I Don't Got To Go To Church

But I Get To

I Don't Got To Take The Time

But I Get To

I Don't Got To Be Baptized

But I Get To

I Don't Got To Change My Life

But I Get To

Get To Turn My Life Around

And Follow Jesus

Get To Change The Way I Think

And Turn To Him

Get To Open Up My Heart

And Let The Holy Spirit In

And Because I'm Born Again

I Get To Worship Him

Yes, I Get To, I Get To

I Don't Got To, But I Get To

I Don't Got To Raise My Hands

But I Get To

I Don't Got To Praise His Name

But I Get To

I Don't Got To Sing And Dance

But I Get To

I Don't Got To Worship Him

But I Get To

Get To Let Patience Have It's Perfect

Work In Me

Get To Love My Lord

Because He First Loved Me

Get To Have Perfect Peace

That Passes Anything I Know

Get To Have That Joy Down In My Soul

Yes, I Get To, I Get To

I Don't Got To, But I Get To

I Don't Got To Pray Today

But I Get To

I Don't Got To Love My Neighbor

But I Get To

I Don't Got To Tell The Truth, But I Get To

I Don't Got To Follow Jesus

But I Get To

Get To Ask And Receive All The Wisdom
That I Need

Get To Understand The Message

Of The Cross

Get To Fight The Good Fight

For The Rest Of My Life

Get To Take The Gospel To The Poor

And Save The Lost

Yes, I Get To, I Get To

I Don't Got To But I Get To\\

I NEED YOU, JESUS

I Walked Into The Stranger's Home

And Sat Down On The Floor

Took A Chance On Coming Here

Thinking I'd Be Bored

The Man Of God Was Interesting

With What He Had To Say

Little Did I Know It Wasn't Ending

When He Prayed

He Said There's Someone Here Tonight

Who Needs Jesus As Your Lord

Speak Up Now, Don't Be Afraid

And You Will Live Forevermore

Someone Spoke Up

And The People Rejoiced

And I Was Somewhat Relieved

Then The Man Of God Said

There's Still Someone

Who Hasn't. . Yet. . Received

And It's Time To Say, I Need You, Jesus,

You Know How Much I Need You

To Come Into My Life

As Everyone Prayed, I Was Feeling Afraid

And Got Closer To The Floor

I Knew It Was Me And I Wanted To Flee

But I Was Too Far From The Door

Then I Looked Into His Eyes

As He Said, "There's Still One More"

So I Said, I Give Up! I Surrender My Life!

Jesus. . Is. . My Lord!

I Felt The Arms Of Satan

Open Wide And Let Me Go

'Cause There Ain't No Power

Under Heaven Or Earth

Like The Power Of The Holy Ghost

His Yoke Is Easy, His Burden, Light

And The Truth Will Set You Free

All You Need To Do Now To Receive

Is Believe ,And It's Time To Say

I Need You, Jesus

You Know How Much I Need You

To Come Into My Life\\

I TURN TO YOU

Jesus, You Could Have Delivered Me

Into The Hands Of The Enemy

But Here I Am, Completely Justified

Not By Anything I've Done

Or Anything I've Tried

And I Turn To You, I Turn To You

I Turn To You, I Turn To You, Lord

Jesus, I Don't Understand

Why I've Been Chosen For This Family

But Still You Came

Giving Me Peace Within

Filling Me With Joy Untold

Leading Me Into The Fold

And I Turn To You, I Turn To You

I Turn To You, I Turn To You, Lord

For You Are Holy, Righteous And True

I Take Up My Cross And Follow You

And You Are Worthy, I Give My Life To You

Lord, I Worship You, I Turn To You

Jesus, Son Of God, You Are

My Life, My Hope, My Breath

You're Everything To Me

You Are God, Whispering In My Ear

Words From Heaven Above

Teaching Me To Love

And I Turn To You, I Turn To You

I Turn To You, I Turn To You, Lord

With All My Heart, With All My Soul

With All My Strength, With All My Mind

In You I Live, And Breath, And Move

Lord, I Worship You, I Turn To You\\

IF EVER I NEEDED YOU

Lord, If Ever I Needed You

If Ever I Needed You, It's Now

Lord, If Ever I Needed Help

If Ever I Needed Help, It's Now

Lord, If Ever I Needed Mercy

If Ever I Needed Mercy, It's Now

Lord, If Ever I Needed Grace

If Ever I Needed Grace, It's Now

All I Have To Offer You

Is All I Have Within Me Now

So I Give You All The Praise

And I Worship You Today

You Are High And Lifted Up

And Your Train Fills The Temple

And I'm Holding On, I'm Holding On

I'm Holding On To You

I'm Holding On, I'm Holding On

I'm Holding On To You

Lord, If Ever I Needed You

If Ever I Needed You, It's Now

Lord, If Ever I Needed Faith

If Ever I Needed Faith, It's Now

Lord, If Ever I Needed Hope

If Ever I Needed Hope, It's Now

Lord, If Ever I Needed Love

If Ever I Needed Love, It's Now

Al I Have To Offer You

Is All I Have Within Me Now

So I Give You All The Praise

And I Worship You Today

You Are High And Lifted Up

And Your Train Fills The Temple

And I'm Holding On, I'm Holding On

I'm Holding On To You\\

MORE THAN I DESERVE

It's More Than I Deserve

I Surrender My Life

My Heart Belongs To You

I'm Walking In The Light

Under The Blood

That Covers Me

You Forgive My Sins

And You Set Me Free

You Know My Name

It's In The Book Of Life

You Know My Name

It's More Than I Deserve

It's More Than I Deserve

I Surrender My Life

My Heart Belongs To You

I'm Walking In The Light

Your Blood

The Redeeming Sacrifice

Transformed Me

From Sin And Death, To Life

Oh, Jesus, You're The Reason I Live

The Truth Has Set Me Free

Amazing Grace For All Eternity

And I Know My Name Is Engraved

In The Palm Of Your Hand

Under The Blood That Covers Me

I Am Delivered, You Set Me Free

You Took The Blinders From My Eyes

And I Can See

It's More Than I Deserve

I Surrender My Life

My Heart Belongs To You

I'm Walking In The Light

Under The Blood

That Covers Me

You Forgive My Sins

And You Set Me Free

You Know My Name

It's In The Book Of Life

You Know My Name

It's More Than I Deserve\\

MY OLD FRIEND

In The Beginning, Before My Life Began

You Were There, Standing By

Every Day

You Made Your Presence Known

To Me, My Old Friend

I Listened To Every Word You Spoke

Your Wisdom Captured Me

In The Darkness Of My Life

In You, I Saw The Light

You Stirred My Soul, My Old Friend

Then It Happened, The Day My Life Began

Born Again When I Believed

It Finally Happened

You Were Knocking On My Door

And There You Were, Standing By

You Said, Say The Words, Don't Be Afraid

Just Speak And You Shall Be Heard

You Said, Say My Name, Profess Your Faith

Just Speak The Name Of Jesus And Live

Forever, And Ever, My Old Friend

It's Been A Long Time

But It Seems Like Yesterday

That You Were There, Standing By

And Every Time We Speak

You Tell Me You Believe In Me

My Old Friend

I Still Listen To Every Word You Speak

Your Wisdom Captures Me

In Every Song We Sing

In Every Song We Sing

You Stir My Soul, My Old Friend

In The Beginning, Before My Life Began

You Were There, Standing By

Every Day, You Make

Your Presence Known

To Me, My Old Friend

You Listen To Every Word I Speak

You Hear Me When I Call

You Love Me And Forgive Me

Lord You Catch Me When I Fall

Again And Again, Jesus

My Old Friend, My Old Friend\\

ONLY JESUS

When I Experience Defeat

I Lay It At Your Feet

You're The Only One

Who Meets My Every Need

And Then You Send Someone My Way

To Brighten Up My Day

And Remind Me That Jesus Loves Me

All Things Became New

When I Gave My Life To You

And I Heard The Holy Spirit Speak To Me

Nothing In This World Could Change

The Way I Live Or Who I Am

Jesus, You're The Only One Who Can

Only Jesus Could Forgive Me Of My Sins

Only Jesus Helped Me Begin Again

Only Jesus Could Breathe New Life Into Me

Only Jesus Could Set Me Free

Only Jesus

And As The Years Have Gone By

I Stopped Asking Why

Because The Why's Never Mattered Anyway

The Only Thing That I Have Left

Is The Spirit Who Gives Me My Next Breath

And I Sing Of His Glory Everyday

All Things Became New

When I Gave My Life To You

And I Heard The Holy Spirit Speak To Me

Nothing In This World Could Change

The Way I Live Or Who I Am

Jesus, You're The Only One Who Can

Only Jesus Could Forgive Me Of My Sins

Only Jesus Helped Me Begin Again

Only Jesus Could Breathe New Life Into Me

Only Jesus Could Set Me Free

Only Jesus

The Lord Is My Shepherd, I Shall Not Want

He Makes Me Lie Down In Green Pastures

He Leads Me Beside The Still Waters

And He Restores My Soul

He Leads Me In The Paths Of Righteousness
All For His Name's Sake

Yea, Though I Walk Through The Valley Of
The Shadow Of Death

I Will Fear No Evil, For You Are With Me

Your Rod And Your Staff, They Comfort Me

And You Prepare A Table For Me In The
Presence Of My Enemies

You Anoint My Head With Oil

And My Cup Runneth Over

Surely Goodness And Mercy Shall Follow Me
All The Days Of My Life

Only Jesus Could Forgive Me Of My Sins

Only Jesus Helped Me Begin Again

Only Jesus Could Breathe New Life Into Me

Only Jesus Could Set Me Free

Only Jesus\\

ONLY ONE

Of All Religions

All Around The World

With All Of Their Beliefs

Their Visions And Their Gods

Only One Had The Power

To Take Back His Life

After Dying On A Cross

He Is The Living Sacrifice

Only One Came From Heaven

Only One Forgave Our Sins

And Because Of Love,

Only One Overcame The Grave

Name Above All Names

Only One Hears Me When I Call

Only One Hears Me When I Stand

And Magnify His Name

Only One Came And Found Me

When I Was So Lost

My Lord, And My God

Jesus, You're The Only One

I Call On Jesus

He Is Worthy To Be Praised

And By Him I Am Saved

From My Enemies

I Call On Jesus

Who Gave Himself For Me

And In My Spirit, I Am Free

And Forgiven For My Sins

I Call On Jesus

No One Else Could Help

No One Else Could Rescue Me

No One Else Could Hear My Cry

Less Of Me, And More Of You

My Lord, Help Me To Not Be

Conformed To This World

And As I Turn To You

From My Selfish Ways

And Look Upon The Cross

And What You Did For Me That Day

Only One Thing Is Left For Me To Do

Take The Message Of The Cross

And Make Disciples Of The Nations

Of The World

Praise The Name Of The Father

Praise The Name Of The Son

Praise The Name Of The Spirit

The Holy One, The Holy One

Only One Hears Me When I Call

Only One Hears Me When I Stand

And Magnify His Name

Only One Came And Found Me

When I Was So Lost

My Lord, And My God

Jesus, You're The Only One\\

PARDON ME

Pardon Me, I Think I've Lost My Way

Pardon Me, Can You Help Me Today

Pardon Me, Please Help Me, I Pray

I'm Not Where I Belong And I Can't Stay

I'm So Lost And I've Been Here

Way Too Long

Paid My Dues, Got The Blues

Everything's Gone Wrong

Something's Gotta Break

Before It's Just Too Late

I'm Not Where I Belong And I Can't Stay

Sing Your Sweet Song Again

That I Heard You Singing With Your Friends

Singing 'bout Jesus, Mercy And Love

I Believe That's What I Need

All The Above

Pardon Me, Lord Jesus

I Repent Of All My Sins

Pardon Me, And Save Me

I Need To Be Born Again

Pardon Me, And In Heaven

Make A Place For Me

And When I Stand Before You Lord

Pardon Me

Pardon Me, My Lord

My God, My Savior

Jesus Make Me Whole

Pardon Me, Deliver Me

From The Accuser Of My Soul

Pardon Me, And Set Me Free

Let The Old Me Pass Away

Lord Jesus, Pardon Me Today

Sing Your Sweet Song Again

That I Heard You

Singing With Your Friends

Singing 'bout Jesus, Mercy And Love

I Believe That's What I Need

All The Above

I Believe That's What I Found

All The Above\\

PLEASE HEAR ME AS I PRAY

I've Come, Lord Jesus

Into This Holy Place

To Offer Up My Life

And Worship You Today

There's Nothing I Did To Deserve

This Amazing Grace

So I Bow Down And Thank You, Lord

Please Hear Me As I Pray

Lord, I Know Your Love For Me

Is More Than I Can See

And I Know You're Here Right Now

Here With Me

My Heart Cries Out, O Lord

Have Mercy On Me

As I Bow Down And Thank You, Lord

Please Hear Me As I Pray

In Your Presence I Find Joy

Joy That Makes Me Strong

In Your Spirit I Find Peace

For My Troubled Soul

In Your Words, I Find Truth

Truth That Sets Me Free

And In Your Church I Find Love

Beyond Compare

Father In Heaven

Hallowed Be Your Name

Your Kingdom Come, Your Will Be Done

Just As It Is In Heaven

Lord, Give Us Our Daily Bread

And Forgive Us Our Sins

As We Forgive Those Who Sin Against Us

Please Hear Me As I Pray

And Lead Us, Now

Not Into Temptation

But Deliver Us, Lord

From The Evil One

For Thine Is The Kingdom

And The Power And The Glory

Please Hear Me As I Pray

As I Pray

I've Come, Lord Jesus

Into This Holy Place

To Offer Up My Life

And Worship You Today

There's Nothing I Did To Deserve

This Amazing Grace

So I Bow Down And Thank You, Lord

Please Hear Me As I Pray

You Are My Strength, Lord

When I Am Weak

You Are The Light Of Life

In My Soul

You Are My Prince Of Peace

In Times Of Trouble

You Are My Lord And My God

Forevermore

Please Hear Me

As I Pray\\

PRAY

Are You Suffering? Let's Pray

Lost And Lonely?

I Can Show You A Better Way

Are You Hurting? Please Stay

Let The Elders Take Their Oil And Pray

In The Name Of Jesus, You Shall Be Healed

The Prayer Of Faith Will Save The Sick

And The Lord Will Raise You Up

In The Name Of Jesus, Rise And Be Healed

The Prayers Of The Righteous

Have Great Power

O Sinner, Confess Your Sins And Pray

Your Sins Will Be Forgiven Here Today

Salvation By None Other; Jesus Is The Way

Let The Elders Take Their Oil And Pray

Are You Doubting? Just Taste And See

That The Lord Is Good

And You Can Be Free

Are You Satisfied? Sing Praise

Abundant Life Is Here For You Today\\

PRODIGAL'S LAMENT

I've Been Down This Road Before

You Think By Now I'd Know The Score

Changing My Mind Is A Hard Thing To Do

When The Truth Is Revealed

I Turn To You

Your Help, Your Love, Your Compassion

Your Mercy

Your Strength, Your Peace, Your Guidance

Your Comfort

Your Righteousness, Holiness, Patience

And Power

Your Grace Is All That I Need

Your Word, Your Joy, Your Forgiveness

Your Goodness

Your Wisdom, Your Presence, Your Spirit

Your Council

Your Faithfulness, Gentleness, Kindness

Your Glory

Your Grace Is Sufficient For Me

Have Mercy On Me

Forgive Me, I Plead

Open My Eyes That I May See

That Jesus Is All That I Need

Quick To Forgive

All My Sins Are Forgiven

Transformed By The Spirit

My Mind Is Renewed

From All My Enemies, I Am Delivered

Your Grace Is All That I Need\\

SEND YOUR ANGELS

Send Your Angels, O Lord, I Pray

To Go Before Me

And Prepare The Way

That My Life Can Be Lived For You

Helping Others To See The Truth

My Help, My Comforter In Time Of Need

You're The Voice I Need To Hear

Come And Speak

Holy Spirit, Teach Me Now

To Surrender My Will

As I Pray

I See Angels All Around

Waiting Patiently For Us To Pray

I Hear Jesus Calling Me,

Saying Child, I'm All You Need

If My People

Who Are Called By My Name

Will Humble Themselves And Pray

Seek My Face

And Turn From Their Ways

I Will Hear Them, Forgive Them

And Heal Their Land

And As I Walk In The Light

Trusting You, Lord

To Work All Things Together

For My Good

Knowing That I Am Not My Own

Jesus, I Belong To You

Jesus, I Belong To You, Hallelujah

Jesus, I Belong To You

Send Your Angels

O Lord, I Pray\\

THANK YOU MY FRIEND

Just Want To Thank You, My Friend

For Answering The Call

Just Wanna Let You Know

How Much You Mean To Us All

You Speak The Word Of Truth

And You Do It All With Joy

It Is Your Heart's Desire

To Serve The Lord

And So, We Say Thank You

We Say Thank You

We Don't Got To, But We Get To

Yes, We Say Thank You

We Say Thank You

And We Pray, Pray, Pray, Pray

Pray, Pray, Pray

Every Day For You

And We Thank The Lord For You

Our Pastor, Our Brother

Our Friend

May Your Family Be Blessed

Beyond Measure

Right Up Until The End

There's A Crown Of Glory Waiting

When Your Work On Earth Is Done

And Jesus Looks At You And Say's

Welcome Home, My Son

And So, We Say Thank You

We Say Thank You

We Don't Got To, But We Get To

Yes, We Say Thank You

We Say Thank You

And We Pray, Pray, Pray, Pray

Pray, Pray, Pray

Every Day For You\\

THANKS TO YOU

Thanks To You, I'm Never Lonely

Thanks To You, All Fear Is Gone

Thanks To You, My Soul Is Satisfied

Thanks To You, My Life

Will Never Be The Same

Thanks To You, I've Come To The Water

Thanks To You, My Sin Is Gone

Thanks To You, My Soul Is Satisfied

Thanks To You

My Life Will Never Be The Same

I Can't Begin To Tell You

What You Mean To Me

I Can't Begin To Tell You

What It Means To Be Set Free

I Can't Begin To Tell You

Just How Much I Need You, Lord

I Can't Begin Another Day

Without You

Thanks To You

I Know My Name Is In The Book

Thank You Jesus

Name Above All Names

Thanks To You, My Soul Is Satisfied

Thanks To You

My Life Will Never Be The Same

Thanks To You

There Is Nothing I Can't Do

Thanks To You

I've Been Redeemed

Thanks To You, My Soul Is Satisfied

Thanks To You

My Life Will Never Be The Same

I Have Peace That Passes Understanding

Joy That Keeps Me Strong

Faith In Jesus Christ

My Lord And Savior All Day Long

What The World Needs To See

Is What I Have Inside Of Me

The Holy Spirit Rising Up In Me

Thanks To You, I Walk In Victory

Thanks To You, I'm Not Ashamed

Thanks To You, My Soul Is Satisfied

Thanks To You

My Life Will Never Be The Same

Thanks To You

I Am Walking In The Light

Thanks To You, I Am Free

Thanks To You

My Soul Is Satisfied

Thanks To You

My Life Will Never Be The Same

I Can't Begin To Tell You

What You Mean To Me

I Can't Begin To Tell You

What It Means To Be Set Free

I Can't Begin To Tell You

Just How Much I Need You, Lord

I Can't Begin Another Day

Without You\\

THIS IS MY HOLY PLACE

Holy, Holy Lord

You Are Holy, Holy Lord

You Alone Are Worthy

Worthy To Be Praised

Here I Am On My Knees

Once Again, Oh Lord

Praying Through

Asking Now For Your Help, Oh Lord

Have Mercy On Me

O God, My God

According To Your Loving Kindness

I Believe You Are Here With Me

And I Know I Am Saved

By Your Grace

Right Now, Right Here

I Can Feel Your Touch

Even Now, This Is My Holy Place

Unending Love That Covers Me

Jesus, Your Power

Delivers Me

Unending Peace

Guards My Heart And My Soul

Receive Me, Now

As I Seek Your Face

In This Place

This Is My Holy Place

Praise The Lord

Praise The Lord

Praise The Name Of The Lord

Let The Name Of The Lord

Be Praised Forevermore

Right Now, Right Here

I Can Feel Your Touch

Even Now, This Is My Holy Place\\

UNTIL JESUS CAME INTO MY LIFE

Take Me Down To The Water

Pick Me Up, And Put Me In

Just Once Is All I'll Ever Need

And You Won't See Me Down Here

Ever Again

Let Me Tell You How It Was For Me

Didn't Think That I'd Survive

No One Seemed To Care

No One Cared To See

Until Jesus Came Into My Life

Until Jesus Came Into My Life

Hallelujah

Until Jesus Came Into My Life

Praise The Lord

No One Seemed To Care

No One Cared To See

Until Jesus Came Into My Life

I Was Trying To Get By

I Was Wanting To Be Free

From The Suffering And Pain

Of This Life Of Misery

No One Seemed To Care

No One Cared To See

Until Jesus Came Into My Life

Take Me Down To The Water

Pick Me Up, And Put Me In

Just Once Is All I'll Ever Need

Cause I'll Be Washed By The Blood

Of The Lamb

He Is My Healer, I Am His Miracle

I Left My Way Of Life

And Changed My Mind

Forgiven For My Sins, I Know

I'm Born Again

Since Jesus Came Into My Life\\

YOU WITH ME

Who Do I Want By My Side

When Trouble Comes And I Can't Hide

Oh, Lord, All I Want Is You With Me

And When My Faith Is Weak

And I Can't Decide

Which Way I Should Go

Oh, Jesus, All I Want Is You With Me

You With Me, Breaking Chains

By The Power Of The Word

You With Me, Standing Strong

Against The Darkness Of The World

You With Me, I'm Not Alone

Let Your Will Be Done In Me

So That Everyone Will See

You With Me

When I Need Wisdom I Don't Have

My Lord, You Don't Hold Back

Oh, Lord, All I Want Is You With Me

And When It Seems That Things

Are Going Well

Even Better Than I Planned

Oh, Jesus, All I Want Is You With Me

I'm Taking Up My Cross

And Following

My Lord, The King Of Kings

Oh, Lord, All I Want Is You With Me

And On The Road Of Suffering

Please, Take Me By The Hand

Oh, Jesus, All I Want Is You With Me

You With Me, Standing Strong

Against The Darkness

Of The World

You With Me, I'm Not Alone

Let Your Will Be Done In Me

So That Everyone Will See

You With Me\\

YOU'RE EVERYTHING TO ME

Why Would Jesus

Take The Punishment

For Something I Did Wrong

How Could Somebody I Don't Know

Know Me

Like He's Been There All Along

Why Do I Deserve

This Amazing Grace?

I Just Want To Fall Down

On My Face

Lord, I Just Want You To Know

You're Everything To Me

Just Want To Thank You Lord

For All That You've Done For Us

Just Want To Praise Your Name

The Name Of Jesus

I Know You're Always There

Letting Us Know You Care, Jesus

And I Just Want You To Know

You're Everything To Me

Just Want To Hear Your Voice

Speak To Me

Reminding Me That You'll

Never Leave Me

Always There, You Always Care

Your Love Is Everlasting

And With All My Heart

With All My Soul

With All My Strength

And With All My Mind

I Will Always Love You

Always Serve You

Always Be Here When You Need Me

I Just Want You To Know

You're Everything To Me\\

CHAPTER 4: WISDOM

4

BE STILL

Be Still And Know That I Am God

As High As The Heavens Are

Above The Earth

So High Is Your Life, Now, With Me

My Thoughts Are With You

And My Spirit Is In You

And My Ways Are Now Yours Forevermore

My Word Came Down

Like The Snow And The Rain

To Bring New Life To All The Earth

My Spirit Is Poured Out Upon All Flesh

And Signs And Wonders Shall Be Seen By All

And All Who Call On My Name

Shall Be Saved

The Alpha And Omega,

The Beginning And The End

The Resurrection And The Life, I Am

The Lamb That Was Slain

The Forgiveness Of Sins

The Promise Of Heaven, I Am\\

EVERY TIME I TURN AROUND

Every Time I Turn Around, I Fall

Jesus, Every Time I Turn Around, I Fall

The Worst Thing I Could Do To You

Is What I Do To You

Every Time I Turn Around, I Fall

And If I Say, I Have No Sin

Then I Stand Against Your Grace

Would Never Be Born Again

Would Never Seek Your Face

Would Never Know The Love You Have

That Covers My Mistakes

Every Time I Turn Around

I Fall

Every Time I Turn Around

You're Here

Jesus, Every Time I Turn Around

You're Here

The Best Thing I Could Do For You

Is Offer Up My Praise

Because Every Time I Turn Around

You're Here

I Know You'll Never Let Me Go

I Feel The Strength Of Your Embrace

I'll Never Be Forsaken

I Feel Your Presence In This Place

Lord, I Thank You For The Love You Have

That Covers My Mistakes

Every Time I Turn To You

I Fall

I Fall At Your Feet, The Feet That Carry Me

When I Am So Weak, So Weak And Weary

The Feet Of Forgiveness, The Feet Of Mercy

You Make Me Strong

You Turn My Sorrow Into Songs

What A Friend We Have In Jesus

All Our Sins And Grief To Bear

What A Privilege To Carry

Everything To God In Prayer

At Your Feet, The Feet Of Forgiveness

The Feet Of Mercy, I Fall At Your Feet

I Fall At Your Feet

I Fall . . .\\

FORTY YEARS BEHIND, RIGHT ON TIME

Tryin' To Get Back To Where I Think I

Shoulda Been By Now

Tryin' To Get Back To Doin' Everything

I Shoulda Done By Now

Tryin' To Make Up For All The Time

I Spent Tryin' To Catch Up

Forty Years Behind; Right On Time

I Might Be Forty Years Behind

But I'm Always On Time

Because What Matters To God Is Today

So, Until I Can Say

I've Arrived, I'm Here To Stay

The Holy Ghost Is Leading The Way

Relax, Be Patient, God Has A Plan

Be A Giver, Not A Taker

And You'll Understand

That The Path You Have Chosen

To Reach You Life's Goals

Has Many A Sharp Turn

And Lots Of Pot Holes

A Purpose For Living

A Passion For Giving

The Power To Live Everyday

These Are The Traits

Of The One Who Is Praying

To The Father In Jesus' Name\\

IF GOD WAS FAIR

It's Not Fair That The Good Ones

Must Suffer And Die

It's Not Fair That My Prayers

Don't Always Keep Them Alive

It's Not Fair That The Wicked

Get To Live Another Day

Tell Me Lord

How Is That Fair?

If God Was Fair

Would He Have Reason To Care For Me?

If God Was Fair

Would He Have Died At Calvary?

If God Was Fair

Would My Sins Be No More?

If God Was Fair

There Would Be No Place In Heaven

For Me

It's Not Fair, How Could He Love

A Sinner Like Me?

Why Would He Let Me Hear His Voice?

Why Would He Speak To Me?

It's Not Fair, Why Would He Send

The Comforter To Me?

It's Not Fair, That At The Cross

His Blood Was Shed For Me

If God Was Fair

Would There Be Mercy For Me?

If God Was Fair

Would There Be Grace

To Set Me Free?

If God Was Fair

Would There Be Peace

To Guard My Heart?

If God Was Fair

There Would Be No Place In Heaven

For Me

It's Not Fair

That Jesus Had To Suffer Such Loss

It's Not Fair That My Sins

Were All Forgiven On The Cross

It's Not Fair That His Prayer

Couldn't Keep Death Away

He Saw My Sins As A Debt

That Only He Could Pay

If God Was Fair

Would He Have Reason To Care For Me?

If God Was Fair

Would He Have Died At Calvary?

If God Was Fair

Would My Sins Be No More?

If God Was Fair

There Would Be No Place In Heaven

For Me

So Lord, I Thank You For Your Mercy

I Thank You For Your Grace

I Thank You For Forgiving Me

Even When I Hid My Face

I Thank You For Your Love

That Changed My Heart And Saved My Soul

None Of This Would Be Mine . . .

If God Was Fair\\

I'M CALLED TO REACH THE GOAL

Where I'm Needed

When I'm Needed

That's The Place I Want To Be

Always Reaching For The Goal

Set In Place At Calvary

Blood Was Shed

Pain Was Suffered

By The Man Of Sorrows

Jesus Took It All

And Set Me Free

I'm Not Reaching For The Calling

I'm Called To Reach The Goal

Jesus Sent The Holy Ghost

To Teach Me All I Need To Know

Forgetting What's Behind

And Pressing Onward

Toward The Prize

Of The Upward Call Of God

In Jesus Christ

How I Get To Where I'm Going

Jesus Is The Way

I Know He's Always With Me

And He Tells Me What I Need To Say

I've Taken Up My Cross

To Follow Jesus Every Day

I Know, With Him

I Can Overcome

Whatever Comes My Way

Gone And Forgotten

That's What Happened To My Sin

Loved And Forgiven

Because I've Been Born Again

The Message Of The Cross

Is The Message That I Preach

Bringing Life And Living Water

To Everyone I Reach

I'm Not Reaching For The Calling

I'm Called To Reach The Goal

Jesus Sent The Holy Ghost

To Teach Me All I Need To Know

Forgetting What's Behind

And Pressing Onward

Toward The Prize

Of The Upward Call Of God

In Jesus Christ\\

I'M MOVING ON

I'm Moving On With Jesus

For Him, I'll Always Go

Where He Needs Me To Go

I'm Moving On With Jesus

He Speaks; I Listen, And Obey

He Didn't Have To Speak

That Day He Saved My Soul

I Felt The Spirit Of The Lord

Change Me And Make Me Whole

He Didn't Let Me Go

'Til He Heard Me Say The Words

I Give Up, I Surrender, Jesus Is My Lord

Absolutely Perfect Submission

Takes Me Beyond All My Dreams

I'm Blessed To Possess This Abundant Life

That Exceedingly Meets All My Needs

Jesus Is The Answer

To Being Forgiven And Free

The Chains Of Sin Were Broken At Calvary

Healing All Manner Of Sickness And Pain

Moving Those Mountains In Jesus Name

Raising The Dead To Life Again

Casting Out All The Demons, And Then

Taking The Gospel To The Poor

So They Can Have Jesus As Their Lord

It's What I'm Called To Do, It's Who I Am

Leaving My Way Of Life Behind

Deciding Again To Change My Mind

And Follow Him Through Thick Or Thin

This Is Why I'm Born Again

I Get To Make A Difference Here

I Get To Make The Message Clear

That God Is Good All The Time

And Jesus Is The Way\\

IN JESUS' NAME

In The Name Of Jesus

You Can Come To The Father

Without Fear, Without Judgment

Without Shame

You Can Stand, You Can Bow

You Can Sit Upon The Throne

As A Joint Heir With Christ

Forevermore

In The Name Of Jesus

All Your Sins Are Forgiven

You Are Changed And You Are Loved

In Jesus' Name

The Holy Spirit Dwells Within You Now

And You Abide In Him

Yes, You Are Saved

By Grace, Through Faith

In Jesus' Name

In The Name Of Jesus

You Can Pray To The Father

Ask Him Anything At All

In Jesus' Name

Make Disciples Of All Nations

Take The Message Of The Cross

Let The Good News Be Heard In Jesus' Name

Heal The Sick, Empty The Beds

Cleanse The Lepers, Raise The Dead

Drive Out Demons

You Have Power In Jesus' Name

Performing Signs And Wonders

By The Spirit Of The Lord

The Truth Shall Set Them Free

In Jesus' Name\\

JESUS IS THE REASON

When I Put Aside The Cares

Of This World

And Look Into His Glorious Word

I Find That Jesus Is The Reason

The Reason For The Season

Today And Every Day

Oh, Jesus Is The Reason

For The Season.

Jesus Is The Reason I Give

When Somebody Asks

Why I Celebrate Christmas

Jesus Is The Reason I Give

When I Put Aside The Past

Full Of Failures And Regrets

And I'm Looking For A Better Way

I Find That Jesus Is The Reason

The Reason For The Season

Today And Every Day

When I Read About Mary And Joseph

And What The Angel Had To Say

I Find That Jesus Is The Reason

The Reason For The Season

Today And Every Day

When I Feel The Holy Spirit Come Upon Me

As We Sing Our Songs Of Praise

I Find That Jesus Is The Reason

The Reason For The Season

Today And Every Day

Oh, Jesus Is The Reason For The Season

Jesus Is The Reason I Give

When Somebody Asks

Why I Celebrate Christmas

Jesus Is The Reason I Give\\

JUST ADD WATER

The Water Began To Rise

But The Church Was Just Too Old

So The People Brought Their Burdens In

To Seal Up That Old Door

Dry Is How We Like It

No Water Should Get In

This Is How We Want It

This Is How It's Always Been

What Do You Do When It's Been So Dry

For So Long You Get To Like It?

What Do You Do When This Wasteland

Feels Like Home?

What Do You Do When There

Ain't Nothin' Left

To Inspire You To Go On?

What Do You Do?

Tell Me, What Do You Do?

It's Been So Long

Since The Children Danced

To Music, Once Inspired

It's Been So Long Since Life Entered

The Songs Of This Old Choir

But Every Now And Then You Know

The River Out Back

Would Send The Water Up To The Door

And Every Now And Then

A Little Water Could Be Seen

Moving Across The Floor

Well, The Children Started

Dancing In The Water

And The Music Was On Fire

Something New Started Happening

In This Church, Long Since Retired

And As The Weeks Went On

It Became The Norm

To Let A Little Water In

'Cause It Felt A Little Like

Heaven Come Down

Compared To Where They'd Been

Well, One Day They Heard The Pastor Say

It's Time We Made A Change

So Bring Your Burdens To The Alter

And Give Them Up In Jesus Name

Well The Burdens Came Up

And The Door Came Down

And The Water Came Rushing In

Baptized In The Holy Ghost

This Church Was Born Again

What Do You Do When It's Been So Dry

For So Long You Get To Like It?

What Do You Do When This Wasteland

Feels Like Home?

What Do You Do When There

Ain't Nothin' Left

To Inspire You To Go On?

What Do You Do?

Tell Me, What Do You Do?

You Just Add Water, Living Water

Holy Water, You Just Add Water

Water Of Life, Healing Water

What Do You Do? . . . You Just Add Water\\

NO LOOKING BACK

I Count My Old Life As Lost

Crucified With Christ

On The Cross

For All My Sins, I Am Forgiven

For All My Sins

He Paid The Cost

No Looking Back

At The Way Things Used To Be

No Looking Back,

Got My Mind On Things Above

No Looking Back

Jesus Is Coming Back

No Looking Back

He's Coming Back For Me

Everything Became New For Me

Since I Asked Jesus In

He Came And He Talked To Me

And Now I'm Born Again

I Count My New Life

As Blessed

God Knows My Name

Jesus Loves Me And Forgives Me

And He Took Away My Sorrow

And My Shame

He Compassion Is Unending

All My Sins

Tossed In The Sea

His Love Has Changed Me

And I'm Becoming

Who He Made Me To Be\\

PEACE, BE STILL, AND KNOW

As The Worshipers Gathered

Together To Pray

I Heard The Holy Spirit Say

Peace, Be Still, And Know

This Message Was Not Given Only To Me

But To Everyone

With The Faith To Believe

Peace, Be Still, And Know

Peace That Passes My Understanding

Now Keeps Me Under Control

Patience Is Having Its Perfect Work

In The Silence Of My Soul

Wisdom That Comes

From Knowing God

And Reaping What I've Sown

Say's, Peace, Be Still

And Know

No Reason To Worry About Today

When You Hear The Holy Spirit Say

Peace, Be Still, And Know

Without Concern For What Words To Speak

Quietly Wait And Think On These

Peace, Be Still, And Know

Ever Present Is He In Times Of Trouble

God Is Our Refuge,

Our Glory And Our Strength

So Fix Your Eyes Now On Jesus

He Is The Author

And Perfecter Of Our Faith

There Is A River Who's Streams Make Glad

The Holy Place

Where The Most High Dwells

And In This River Is The Tree Of Life

Saying, Peace, Be Still And Know\\

PEOPLE CHANGE BUT GOD STAYS THE SAME

Maybe You Won't Miss Me When I'm Gone

Cause All You See

Is All That I've Done Wrong

You Closed Your Heart

And Changed Your Mind

And Decided I'm Not Worth Your Time

Maybe You Won't Miss Me When I'm Gone

Loving God And Enjoying Life

Should Be All That Really Matters

Attitudes, Beatitudes

I Think I'll Take The Latter

I Found Someone

Who Changed My Life

My Lord And Savior, Jesus Christ

People Change But God Stays The Same

Maybe You Won't Miss Me When I'm Gone

But I Hope That You'll Forgive Me

For All That I've Done Wrong

Don't Let Your Heart Be Troubled

Just Turn To Him And Pray

'Cause It's Not About Me

It's Not About You

Jesus Is The Way

Loving God And Enjoying Life

Should Be All That Really Matters

Attitudes, Beatitudes

I Think I'll Take The Latter

I Found Someone

Who Changed My Life

My Lord And Savior, Jesus Christ

People Change But God Stays The Same

Maybe You Won't Miss Me

When I'm Gone

But If You Do, Don't Worry

'Cause It Won't Be That Long

We'll Find Our Way To Jesus

In The Twinkling Of An Eye

When He Comes Again

And We Meet Him In The Sky

Loving God And Enjoying Life

Should Be All That Really Matters

Attitudes, Beatitudes

I Think I'll Take The Latter

I Found Someone

Who Changed My Life

My Lord And Savior, Jesus Christ

People Change But God Stays The Same

He Never Changes

He Shed His Blood For Me At Calvary,

He Never Changes

His Love For Me   Covers All My Sins

He Never Changes, He Conquered Death
And Rose Up From The Grave

People Change, But God Stays The Same\\

PURE RELIGION

Every Good And Perfect Gift Is From Above

Coming Down From The Father Of Lights

There Is No Variation

Or Shadow Of Turning

I'm So Glad I Met My Savior, Jesus Christ

I Will Always Do What's Right

'Cause I'm Walking In The Light

And Jesus Gives Me Strength To Persevere

I'm A Doer Of The Word

Not By Power, Not By Might

But By The Spirit When I'm Needed

I Am Here

This Pure Religion Isn't Living

By A Special Set Of Man-Made Rules

But It Is Wisdom From The Lord, Our God

It Is Good News We Can Use

This Pure Religion Isn't Vain

It Is Love In Jesus Name

When Pure Religion Gets Ahold Of You

You Will Never Be The Same

Quick To Hear, Slow To Speak

Slow To Anger, I Have Learned

That The Righteousness Of God

Has Made Me Whole

All The Bad That Is Behind Me

Is Replaced, Now, By The Word

And Implanted In My Blood-Bought Soul

With Ears To Hear And Eyes To See

Since The Day He Set Me Free

I'm So Thankful For This Pure Religion

He Gives Me Words When I Speak

And The Grace That I Need

To Do His Will In The Light

Of Pure Religion\\

SIMPLY ANOINTED

Used To Think That I Would Find

That One Thing

That Would Give Me Peace Of Mind

One Step To Move Me Up

And Put Me At The Head Of The Line

Then I Found Something So Profound

A Simple Truth That Took Me By Surprise

When I'm Weak, He Is Strong

His Grace Is Sufficient

It's Christ In Me, Not I

Simply Anointed

With The Power Of God

Who Lived And Who Died

And Who Rose From The Dead

Just To Be With Me

Simply Anointed

With The Power Of God

Simply Giving Up All That I Have

In Service To My King

Simply Surrendered

All To Jesus, My Lord

Simply Anointed By The King

The King Of Kings

Now I Know That I Have Found

That One Thing That Gives Me

Peace Of Mind

One Step, Beyond Myself

Where Jesus Comes

And Tells Me We Are Fine

This I Know To Be True

A Simple Truth

That Takes Away My Pride

When I'm Weak, He Is Strong

His Grace Is Sufficient

It's Christ In Me, Not I

Manifested In Flesh

Justified By The Spirit

The Angels Are Singing His Song

He Knows All Our Stories

Received Up In Glory

He Reigns Forevermore

Simply Anointed \\

SOMETIMES THE SCARS DON'T GO AWAY

Just As The Rain Falls Down

On Saints, And On Sinners

On The Same Day, In The Same Way

Trouble Comes, Yes, It Does

But When I Fall On My Knees

Saying, Jesus, Help Me, Please

On The Same Day, In The Same Way

He Speaks To Me, Yes, He Does

He Says, Let Not Your Heart Be Troubled

All These Things Are For Your Good

Believe In Me

I Will Deliver You

And As You Seek My Face

The Sufficiency Of Grace

Means Sometimes

Sometimes The Scars Don't Go Away

I Am Crucified With Christ

And He Has Given Me New Life

On The Same Day

All My Sins Were Washed Away

He Set Me Free

And In The Palms Of His Hands

My Name Has Been Engraved

On The Same Day, In The Same Way

Under The Blood, Under The Blood

Such Great Revelations I Have Had

A Humbling I Needed

So That I Don't Get All Caught Up

In My Selfishness And Greed

And As I Pleaded, Take This Pain Away

I've Had It Way Too Long

He Said My Grace Is Sufficient

In Your Weakness, I Am Strong

Just As The Rain Falls Down

On Saints, And On Sinners

On The Same Day, In The Same Way

Trouble Comes, Yes, It Does

But, Just As The Rain Falls Down

On Saints, And On Sinners

On The Same Day, In The Same Way

Jesus Comes, Yes, He Does

Oh, Those Nails On That Cross

Pierced The Hands That Save The Lost

Those Were The Nails Prepared For Me

That Glorious Day

Yes, Those Nails On That Cross

Shed The Blood That Paid The Cost

And Sometimes

The Scars Don't Go Away\\

WHENEVER I PULL A JONAH I GET A WHALE

Oh, It Feels So Good To Trust In The Lord,

Yes, It Feels So Good To Trust In The Lord

Oh, It Feels So Good To Trust

In The Lord, My God

My Jesus Is Faithful To Me

For As Long As I Recall

I Get Up And Then I Fall

This World Has Not Been Good To Me At All

On This Roller Coaster Ride

Sometimes I Feel Like I Could Die

'Cause Whenever I Pull A Jonah

I Get A Whale

It's Not A Whale Of A Good Time

When You're Steppin' Off The Line

Trying To Please Everybody But The Lord

Oh, It's Best Not To Fret

When He's Got Things For You To Do

'Cause Whenever You Pull A Jonah

You Get A Whale

Once Was Lost But Now I'm Found

Was Blind But Now I See

This Is What My God Has Done For Me

Taking Up My Cross

Is The Only Way For Me

'Cause Whenever I Pull A Jonah

I Get A Whale

If You Trust In The Lord

You Won't Pull A Jonah

And You Won't Get A Whale\\

WHO IS THIS MAN

Who Is This Man

That Died For Me At Calvary

Who Is This Man

That Rose Up From The Grave

Is He Only The Man We See

In Those Paintings Of Old

Or Is Jesus Someone I Can Know

Who Is This Man

Does He Laugh Out Loud

Does He Always Have A Song

When He Sees Someone In Need

Would He Ask Me To Come Along

And As I Pray For Them

Will He Whisper In My Ear

I've Given You Everything They Need

Who Is This Man

He Said, I Am, I Am In The Father

And You Are In Me

And I Am, I Am In You

So Trust And Obey And Believe

Now, Who Can Tell Me

That I'm Wrong About Jesus

Who Can Tell Me

That I'm Crazy To Believe

When I Speak In His Name

The Power That Comes Forth

Is Evidence That Jesus Is With Me

I Always Stop To Listen When He Speaks

He's My Lord, He's My Strength

When I Am Weak

His Wisdom Takes Me Far Beyond

Where I Thought That I Would Be

Yes, Jesus Put His Spirit In Me

Who Is This Man?\\

CHAPTER 5:
IN MEMORIAM

5

AT THE GATES OF HEAVEN

In The Movies Of Long Ago

When You Hear A Bell Ring

An Angel Gets Their Wings

But We Know Better,

'Cause He's Been There

Jesus Walks The Streets Of Gold

In All His Glory

And He'll Be Standing

At Those Gates Made Of Pearl

He'll Be Greeting All The Saints

Into His World

We Have A Home There

We Have A Mansion

And I Know I'll See Him There

At The Gates Of Heaven

You Don't Have To Worry About Dying

Jesus Conquered Death; I'm Testifying

New Life Is Here For You

Right Here, Right Now, Today

Loved And Forgiven; You Can Be Saved

All Of Heaven Gives A Shout

When A Sinner Calls His Name

Saying, Jesus Is My Lord

And I've Been Born Again

That's All It Takes For You To Enter In

And I Know You'll See Him There

At The Gates Of Heaven

Let Not Your Heart Be Troubled

It's What Jesus Said To Do

I've Prepared A Place For You, He Said

And I Will Be There, Too

Jesus Sacrificed

To Give Us Eternal Life

Just Turn And Say To Him

I Believe

All Of Heaven Gives A Shout

When A Sinner Calls His Name

Saying, Jesus Is My Lord

And I've Been Born Again

That's All It Takes For You To Enter In

And I Know You'll See Him There

At The Gates Of Heaven

And He'll Be Standing

At Those Gates Made Of Pearl

He'll Be Greeting All The Saints

Into His World

We Have A Home There

We Have A Mansion

And I Know I'll See You There

At The Gates Of Heaven

Yes' I Hope I'll See You There

At The Gates Of Heaven\\

FOREVER

Your Life, Unseen

Is Now Hidden

With Christ In God

To Be Revealed With Him In Glory

When He Appears

And We Shall All See

And We Shall All Dance

And We Shall All Sing

Glory To The Lamb

And We Shall Honor Him

And We Shall Worship Him

Jesus Christ, The King

Worthy Of All Praise

Forever

You Have Entered

Into His Presence

Into His Rest

Forever Thankful

For All That He Has Done

Forever We Are Blessed

And We Shall All See

And We Shall All Dance

And We Shall All Sing

Glory To The Lamb

And We Shall Honor Him

And We Shall Worship Him

Jesus Christ, The King

Worthy Of All Praise

Forever\\

I FOUND MYSELF IN GLORY

Bad Days Come And Go

This One Seemed To Stay

I Prayed, And I Remembered

What I Heard Jesus Say

Let Not Your Heart Be Troubled

Believe In Me

In My Father's House There's A Mansion

Just For You

I Found Myself In Glory

And I've Never Felt This Good

Seeing Now, My Story

Had Purpose For My Soul

I Have Joy So Much Greater, Now

Love So Much Deeper

Life More Abundant

Than I Have Ever Known

This Place Is So Magnificent

Created Just For Me

By The King Of Glory

Whose Face I Now See

Everlasting Life, Everlasting Love

Everlasting Thanks And Praise

To My Lord And My God

Everlasting Life, Everlasting Love

Everlasting Thanks And Praise

To God, Who Welcomes Me Home

There Are Thoughts I'll Never Have Up Here

Words I'll Never Say

No Sorrow, Grief Or Sadness

No Suffering Or Pain

Empty Mansions, Here, Are Waiting

For More To Join My Praise

And We'll All Sing Together

As We Praise His Holy Name\\

I'LL BE LEAVING HERE WALKING IN THE LIGHT

When It's Time For Me To Move On

From This World

I'll Be Leaving Here Walking In The Light

Ain't No Darkness On The Other Side

Waiting There For Me

I'll Be Leaving Here Walking In The Light

Oh I'll Be Leaving Here

Walking In The Light, Hallelujah

I'll Be Leaving Here Walking In The Light

Praise The Lord

Because Down Deep In My Soul

I Have The Light Of Life

I'll Be Leaving Here Walking In The Light

No More Pain, No More Sorrow

No More Misery For Me

I'll Be Leaving Here Walking In The Light

Ain't No Lake Of Fire For Me

And No Gnashing Of The Teeth

I'll Be Leaving Here Walking In The Light

The Only Fire I Expect To See

Is The Fire In His Eyes

As Jesus Says

Welcome Home My Child

Yes, I'll Be Leaving Here

Walking In The Light

Oh I'll Be Leaving Here

Walking In The Light, Hallelujah

I'll Be Leaving Here Walking In The Light

Praise The Lord

Because Down Deep In My Soul

I Have The Light Of Life

I'll Be Leaving Here Walking In The Light\\

I'LL SEE YOU IN HEAVEN

Joy Unspeakable

That's What You Brought To Me

And I Know There Are So Many Here

That Know Just What I Mean

Your Sweet Smile, I'll Never Forget

And Those Wonderful Hugs

They Were Just The Best

I'm Gonna Miss You

You Know I Will

I'm Gonna Miss You

But I Know In Heaven, In Heaven

There's A Place Prepared Just For You

And Jesus, Jesus Is There

He's There With You

And It Won't Be Long, I'll Be Right Along

To Sit And Talk With You

And Tell You Just What You Mean To Me

A Sweet, Sweet Spirit, And A Faith So True

And In Your Eyes, The Light Of Life

You Changed My World And Gave Me Hope

Hope Of A Better Life

Your Sweet Smile, I'll Never Forget

And Those Wonderful Hugs

They Were Just The Best

And Because Of You

I Sing Halleluiah

I'm Gonna Miss You

You Know I Will

I'm Gonna Miss You

I'll See You In Heaven\\

IN DUE TIME

Redeemed By His Blood

I Found Mercy Just For Me

Covered By His Love

Jesus Came, He Came To Me

And In Due Time I Beheld

The Beauty Of The Lord

And Jesus Saved My Soul In Due Time

In Due Time We Shall All Behold

The Beauty Of The Lord

In Due Time We Shall All

Inquire In His Temple

In Due Time, Every Knee Shall Bow

And Every Tongue Confess

That Jesus Is The Lord Of All

And All Who Believe

Shall Be Received

In Due Time

Surrendering My Life

Was An Easy Victory

He Was There All The Time

Waiting Patiently For Me

And In Due Time I Called His Name

And In My Heart, I Believed

And Jesus Rescued Me

In Due Time

He's My Light And My Salvation

Whom Shall I Fear?

He's The Strength Of My Life

Even Now, He's With Me, Here

And In Due Time, This One Thing

That I Desire, I Shall Have

I Shall Dwell In His House Forever

In Due Time\\

NOW AND FOREVER

The Passing Of The Brethren

The Passing Of A Friend

The Passing Of A Loved One

Doesn't Mean The End For Them

Eternity Is Promised Those

Who Have The Light Of Life

And As The Light Shines In The Darkness

Jesus Christ Has Won The Fight

Now And Forever

I Am Worshiping The King

Now And Forever, My Heart Shall Sing

Praises To My Savior

For All He's Done For Me

And For The Life He Gave For Me To Live

I Will Live For All Eternity

In Him I Live Now, Forever

Because He Gave His Life

So I Could Live Forever In His Sight

He Set Me Free

And He Saved Me

From The Power Of Death And Sin

And It All Began

When I Was Born Again

Yes, It All Began

When I Was Born Again

Now And Forever

I Shall Walk The Streets Of Gold

Now And Forever

I Never Shall Grow Old

Heaven Is My Home, Now

Prepared By Him, For Me

And I Hope You Get To Know Him

I Hope You'll Be Here With Me\\

SURPRISED BY JOY

Sometimes I Didn't See

Everything That I Should See

Sometimes I Couldn't Hear

Everything You Said To Me

And My Knees Just Wouldn't Let Me

Get Down, Anymore, To Pray

The Aches And Pains Just Never Went Away

But I Have A Friend In Jesus

And My Help Comes From The Lord

I Know, And I Believe

He Is My Lord Forevermore

He Heard Me When I Prayed

And You Know I'll Be All Right

'Cause I've Opened My Eyes

In Paradise

Surprised By Joy

Oh, What A Beautiful Place To See

Surprised By Joy

Hear Jesus Calling Me

Surprised By Joy

I Will Fall Down On My Knees

To Worship And Adore Him

I'll Dance And Shout Before Him

Forever Will I Stay

Surprised By Joy

The Way, The Truth, The Life

I've Come To Know What It's All About

Jesus Set Me Free

And I Will Dance And I Will Shout

If You Believe, Then There's A Place For You

And Jesus Is The Way

And Just Like Me, Forever Will You Stay

Surprised By Joy\\

TIL YOU CAME KNOCKING

The Preacher Showed Up At The Door

After My First Heart Attack

It's A Scary Thing To Contemplate The End

He Told Me About Jesus

And What He's Done For Me

And That's The Day That I Was Born Again

Til You Came Knocking

I Was A Dead Man Walking

Living Just To Live Until I Die

Hanging On To All I Had

Was All That I Could Do

'Cause There Ain't No Picking And Grinning

When The Life That You've Been Living

Is A Lie

Many More Heart Attacks, I've Had

And A Tumor On My Brain

It's Enough To Make A Bigger Man Insane

But In Christ, I Live And Breathe

And There's A Place For Me In Heaven

I Know This

'Cause I've Had The Tour

I've Seen The Streets Of Gold

And The Sky Is Bright, Like Silver

And The Mansions Are Big And Bright

And Grand

And I Stood By Jesus Side

As We Looked Upon That Gate

And I Know That's Where I'll Be

To Shake Your Hand\\

WELCOME HOME

You Were On His Mind In The Garden

When Jesus Prayed, Thy Will Be Done

And When He Hung Upon The Cross,

It Was For You

For The Joy Set Before Him

Was That One Day He Would Say

Welcome Home

My Good And Faithful Friend

Welcome Home, My Child

Let The Angels Gather 'Round

There's Rejoicing In All Of Heaven

Because Of You

Welcome Home, Welcome Home

I've Got A Place Prepared For You

Where We Can Sit And Talk

Welcome Home

Since We Met, My Child

I Want You To Know

The Pleasure's Been All Mine

What We Have Here Can't Be Measured

Not By Space, Not By Time

I Was There When You Were Born

And My Love Will Never End

Welcome Home

My Good And Faithful Friend

Lord, I Know You Made A Place For Me

A Place In Paradise

And It's Oh, So Nice

To Be Here With You

And Up And Down The Streets Of Gold

The Mansions Are Prepared

And Together We'll Have

The Best Times Of Our Lives\\

WHEN THE CALL CAME IN

When The Call Came In, I Was Ready

I Knew His Time On Earth

Would Soon Come To An End

When The Call Came In, I Was Ready

I Knew The Time Had Come

For The Lord To Take Him Home

When The Call Came In

I Knew What I Would Hear

He'd Been So Sick

For Such A Long, Long Time

When The Call Came In

I Knew Before I Answered

My Momma Said, Son

Could You Come Right Over Here

I Walked Into The House

And Went Into His Room

I Saw The Empty Vessel

That He Had Left Behind

I Know He Knew Where He Was Going

He Told Me So, So Many Times

I Put My Hand Upon His Head

And Said Goodbye

Lift Jesus Up And You'll Be Ready

Lift Jesus Up

O Death, Where Is Your Sting

Lift Jesus Up, He's Willing And Ready

He Conquered Death

So That You Can Be Born Again

He Wants To Heal You

Change You, Sanctify You

Love You, Forgive You, Justify You

Nail Your Sins Upon The Tree

Salvation Has Come

To Set You Free\\

CHAPTER 6: PRAISE

6

CASTING ALL MY CARES UPON YOU

I'm Casting All My Cares Upon You, Lord

For You Care For Me

Jesus, You Care For Me

Jehovah Jireh, God Who Provides

I'm Casting All My Cares Upon You

Jehovah Shalom, God Who Gives Me Peace

I'm Casting All My Cares Upon You

Jehovah Rapha, God Who Heals

I'm Casting All My Cares Upon You

Jehovah Nissi, The Banner Over Me

The Banner Over Me Is Love

I'm Casting All My Cares Upon You, Lord

For You Care For Me

Jesus, You Care For Me\\

GIVE HIM ALL THE GLORY

I've Got To Lift My Hands, Praise His Name

And Give Him All The Glory

Jesus Saved My Soul

Jesus Made Me Whole

Jesus Is My King, Jesus Is My Friend

God's Been So Good To Me, Forgiven Me

I Give Him All The Glory

God's Been So Good To Me

He Healed Me

And I Give Him All The Glory

God's Been So Good To Me

He Saved Me

And I Give Him All The Glory

Jesus Saved My Soul

Jesus Made Me Whole

Jesus Is My King, Jesus Is My Friend\\

HANDS THAT NEVER FAIL

Such A Treasure I Have Found

In This Place Where Love Abounds

All Things Measured Gone Away

All Things Beautiful Are Here To Stay

Where Jesus Reigns As King

Creator Of All Things

I Lift My Voice In Praise

To Honor Him

The Blood He Shed For Me

As He Died On Calvary

Took Away My Sins When I Believed

Prepared For Me By Hands That Never Fail

Every Board In Place

Every Cut, And Every Nail

A Work Of Love Created Just For Me

By Jesus Christ, My Lord, My Victory

Took My Place Upon The Tree

Took My Sins And Set Me Free

Gave Me Faith And I Believed

Entered The Kingdom On My Knees

Where Jesus Reigns As King

Creator Of All Things

I Lift My Voice In Praise To Honor Him

The Blood He Shed For Me

As He Died On Calvary

Took Away My Sins When I Believed

My Life Is In His Hands

Everything I Do And Who I Am

I've Learned To Trust, I've Learned To Love

These Hands That Never Fail\\

HIS PRAISE ENDURES FOREVER

I Will Give Thanks To The Lord

With My Whole Heart

In The Company Of The Upright

I Will Give Thanks To The Lord

With My Whole Heart, In The Congregation

Great Are The Works Of The Lord

Known By All Who Delight In Them

His Praise Endures Forever!

Holy And Awesome Is His Name!

Full Of Splendor And Majesty

And His Righteousness Endures

Forever, And Ever

The Lord Is Gracious And Merciful

His Works Will Be Remembered

His Covenant Is Forever

His Praise Endures Forever!

I HAVE A REASON TO REJOICE

I Have Faith, Lord

To Move My Mountain

I Have Wisdom

To Change My World

I Have Water

From You're Holy Fountain

I Have The Power

The Power Of Your Word

Let Me See Into The Spirit

Let Me Hear You're Gentle Voice

Let Me Serve You Now With Gladness

As I Clearly Have A Reason To Rejoice

Holy, Holy Are You, Lord

You Are Worthy To Be Praised

Hear My Prayer, Lord, Hear My Cry

Hear My Prayer

As I Call Upon Your Name

Let Me See Into The Spirit

Let Me Hear You're Gentle Voice

Let Me Serve You Now With Gladness

As I Clearly Have A Reason To Rejoice

Your Name Is Holy, Your Word Is True

In You I Live, In You I Breathe

In You I Move

I Have A Reason For Everything I Do

And Everything I Do Is For You

Let Me See Into The Spirit

Let Me Hear You're Gentle Voice

Let Me Serve You Now With Gladness

As I Clearly Have A Reason To Rejoice\\

I WANT TO PRAISE HIM

Every Time I Think About

What Jesus Did For Me

I Want To Praise Him, I Want To Praise Him

Every Time I Think About

What Jesus Did For Me

I Want To Thank Him, I Want To Praise Him

Praise Him In His Sanctuary

I Want To Praise Him

Praise Him For His Mighty Power

I Want To Praise Him

Praise Him For His Mighty Acts

I Want To Praise Him

Praise Him For His Excellent Greatness

I Want To Praise Him

Every Time I Think About

What Jesus Did For Me

I Want To Praise Him, I Want To Praise Him

Every Time I Think About

What Jesus Did For Me

I Want To Thank Him, I Want To Praise Him

Praise Him With The Sound Of The Trumpet

I Want To Praise Him

Praise Him With The Psaltery And The Harp

I Want To Praise Him

Praise Him With The Tumbrel

And The Dance

I Want To Praise Him

Praise Him, Let Everybody Praise Him

I Want To Praise Him

Every Time I Think About

What Jesus Did For Me

I Want To Praise Him\\

IT'S NICE TO GET UP IN THE MORNING

Oh, It's Nice To Get Up In The Morning

As The Sun Begins To Shine

It Makes Me Think Of God Above

And All That He Provides

He Gives Me Love, He Gives Me Life

As Holy As Is His

It's Not By My Own Efforts

But By Grace Through Faith It Is

Oh, I Give Him All The Praise

And I Give Him All The Glory

And I Give Him All The Honor That Is Due

He Is Worthy Of The Praise

He Is Worthy Of The Glory

He Is Worthy Of This Life I Live Anew

He Was Knocking On The Door

And I Did Open It And See

That Jesus Is A Friendly Sort

To Come And Dine With Me

He Told Me That He Loves Me

Of My Sins, He Does Not Know

And On That Day, He Promised Me

That He Would Never Go

Oh, It's Nice To Get Up In The Morning

When The Son Is On My Mind

It Makes Me Think On Things Above

And Missions I Will Find

I See The World Around Me

His Creation, Through And Through

Is Calling From The Darkness

For To See The Light Of Truth

Oh, I've Seen The Light That Shines

Upon The Faces Of His Own

The People Of The Kingdom

That Shall Never Be Alone

I've Seen Them Working In The Fields

To Bring The Harvest In

I've Seen Them Work With All Their Might

I've Seen The Fishers Of Men

Oh, Through His Death He Gave Me

This New Life Abundantly

And By The Resurrection Of The Truth

I Am Set Free

'Tis True That Jesus Is The Life

'Tis True He Is The Way

To The Father We Can Boldly Come

In Jesus Name, To Pray\\

LET GOD ARISE

Take Us, Change Us, Heal Us, Deliver Us

Restore Us, Renew Us

Revive Us, And Send Us

You Are The Lord

My Savior And My God

Jesus, Arise In Me

Let God Arise

And His Enemies Be Scattered

Jesus, Arise In Me

Let God Arise

Filled With The Holy Ghost And Fire

Let God Arise

Praying In The Holy Ghost With Power

Let God Arise

You Are The Lord, My Savior And My God

Jesus, Arise In Me, Let God Arise\\

LIFE STARTS NOW

Despised And Rejected

On The Cross

He Bled For Me

Punished For My Sins

He Died At Calvary

This Man Of Sorrows Took My Shame

Acquainted With Grief He Took My Pain

Then Rising From The Grave

He's The Banner Over Me

The Resurrection And The Life

He Set Me Free

His Love Is Everlasting

And His Word Is In My Soul

I'm Free At Last, I'm Free

Life Starts Now! And I Believe

It's What I Live For, It's What He Died For

Life Starts Now! And I Receive

The Holy Ghost And Power

In This Very Hour

Thanks Be Unto You, Lord

And Praise Be Multiplied

Blessed Be The God And Father

Of Our Lord, Jesus Christ\\

PRAISE YE THE LORD

Praise Ye The Lord

In The Firmament Of His Power

Praise Ye The Lord

In His Sanctuary

Praise Him For His Mighty Acts

Praise His Excellent Greatness

Praise Him With The Sound Of The Trumpet

Praise The Lord

Praise Ye The Lord

With The Psaltery And The Harp

Praise Ye The Lord

With The Tumbrel And The Dance

Praise Him With Stringed Instruments

Praise Him With The Cymbals

Let Everything That Has Breath

Praise The Lord\\

SINS DON'T STICK TO BLOOD

Purged By The Blood Of The Son Of God

The One Who Took My Place

All My Guilt Has Been Removed

And I'm Saved By Grace Through Faith

Jesus Is The King Who Came To

Rescue Me From Death And Sin

And He Set Me Free

'Cause Sins Don't Stick To Blood

Why Am I So Afraid?

Is There Something In This World

That Will Stick To My Soul?

Why Am I So Afraid? Do I Believe The Truth

That God's In Control?

Why Am I So Afraid?

Is There Something In This World

That Will Stick To My Soul?

Why Am I So Afraid? Do I Believe The Truth

That Sins Don't Stick To Blood ?

I'm Covered By His Love

And I'm Redeemed By His Blood

With All My Sins Forgiven On The Cross

Not By Anything I've Done

Jesus Did It All In Love

And He Set Me Free

'Cause Sins Don't Stick To Blood

Why Am I So Afraid?

Is There Something In This World

That Will Stick To My Soul?

Don't Taste This, Don't Touch That

Hide My Eyes, Make A Pact

To Know The Evil From The Good

This Is Not The Life That God Has

Given Me The Will To Live

It Keeps Me From The Truth

That Sins Don't Stick To Blood

I'm Walking In The Light

There Can Be No Doubt About

What I Believe

Nevermore To Be Afraid

Jesus Overcame The Grave

And Sins Don't Stick To Blood\\

THE GREATEST THING

The Greatest Thing About Joy

Is Not The Gifts That I Receive

The Greatest Thing About Joy

Is Not What This World Believes

The Greatest Thing About Joy

The Greatest Thing I See

Is The Gift Of My Salvation

And The Joy It Brings To Me

I've Got Joy That Makes My Strong

I've Got Joy That Gives Me Peace

I've Got Joy That Makes Me Happy

When Joy Is What I Need

I've Got Joy Going In

I've Got Joy Coming Out

I've Got The Joy Of The Lord

And It Makes Me Want To Shout

The Greatest Thing About Jesus

Is Not The Gifts That I Receive

The Greatest Thing About Jesus

Is Not What This World Believes

The Greatest Thing About Jesus

The Greatest Thing I See

Is The Gift Of My Salvation

And The Joy He Brings To Me

The Greatest Thing About Heaven

Is Not The Gifts That I'll Receive

The Greatest Thing About Heaven

Is Not What This World Believes

The Greatest Thing About Heaven

The Greatest Thing I See

It's The Gift Of My Salvation

And The Joy It Brings To Me

I've Got Joy That Makes My Strong

I've Got Joy That Gives Me Peace

I've Got Joy That Makes Me Happy

When Joy Is What I Need

I've Got Joy Going In,

I've Got Joy Coming Out

I've Got The Joy Of The Lord

And It Makes Me Want To Shout\\

THE VICTORY IS CHRIST IN ME

Soul And Spirit Divided Now

By A Simple Truth

The Word Of God Is Powerful

The Word Of God Is True

And Truth Revealed Requires

That I Decide Between The Two

The Soul Says, I Don't Know

And The Spirit Says, I Do

In Christ I Live, In Christ I Breathe

In Christ I Move, And Have My Being

This Simple Truth Has Set Me Free

The Victory Is Christ In Me

I Sat There In My Misery Feeling Oh, So Sick

The Pain Was So Intense

I Didn't Know If I Would Live

And As I Sat There Feeling Like

I Might Die From This

The Word Of God Came Through My Mind

And Then I Was Convinced

In Christ I Live, In Christ I Breathe

In Christ I Move, And Have My Being

This Simple Truth Has Set Me Free

The Victory Is Christ In Me

Still In Pain, I Stood Right Up

And Said, Enough Of This

Got Things To Do, I'm Going Out

And To The Devil I Shook My Fist

In Jesus Name I Am Now Healed

This, I Have Decided

I Am An Overcomer And You Are Just A Liar

The Simple Truth Is, God Is Love

No Matter What You Do

But Faith Requires Action

It's A Wonderful, Powerful Tool

And As You Choose To Stand

And Believe His Word Is True

No Weapon Formed Against You

Will Ever Make It Through

In Christ I Live, In Christ I Breathe

In Christ I Move, And Have My Being

This Simple Truth Has Set Me Free

The Victory Is Christ In Me\\

THERE IS A NAME

There Is A Name

Above All Names

How Great, How Great

Is That Name

The Blind Shall See

The Deaf Shall Hear

The Lame Shall Walk

In That Name

The Dead Shall Rise

The Sick Made Well

At The Mention Of That Name

There Is A Name

Above All Names

How Great, How Great

Is That Name

And In That Name

Lives Are Changed

Sins Are Forgiven

In That Name

And In That Name,

You Can Be Saved

Just Believe And Call That Name

There Is A Name

Above All Names

How Great, How Great

Is That Name

There Is Power In The Name Of Jesus

Healing In The Name Of Jesus

How Great, How Great

Is That Name

There Is Mercy In The Name Of Jesus

Forgiveness In The Name Of Jesus

How Great, How Great

Is That Name\\

CHAPTER 7: WORSHIP

7

HE MADE ME HOLY

With The Cross Behind Me

I Am Now Holy

Not Because Of Anything I Do

My Holiness Is The Gospel Of Grace

That Created Me Anew

He Made Me Holy

When I Was Not Worthy

He Made Me Righteous

When I Was Wrong

He Justified Me When I Was Guilty

And He Opened My Eyes

When I Was Blind

It Is By Design

That I Am Finally

Free From Adam's Sin

And Now I Am Walking With Jesus

And I Am Born Again

He Brought Me Into

The Light Of Life

Healed My Body

When I Was In Pain

Renewed My Mind

When I Was Crazy

Now I'm Crazy For Jesus

All The Time

He Made Me Holy

When I Was Not Worthy

He Made Me Righteous

When I Was Wrong

He Justified Me

When I Was Guilty

And He Opened My Eyes

When I Was Blind\\

I FOUND MY PLACE

To Be Here, Jesus, In This Place With You

To Be Here, Jesus

To Pray And Worship You

Forever Changes Me, Forever Changes Me

To Be Here, Jesus, It's Where I Need To Be

Here Before You, Finding Everything I Need

I Hear You Calling Me

I Hear You Calling Me

To Be Here With You

Redeemed By The Blood

Born Again, You Breathed Life Into Me

Old Things Have Passed Away

All Things Have Become New

So Glad I Found My Place Here With You

Thank You, Jesus

You Took My Place On The Cross

Thank You, Jesus

If Not For You I Would Be Lost

I Found My Place In You

I Found My Place In You\\

IT'S YOU

Holy Father, Precious Jesus

The World Needs To Know

You Came And Found Me When I Was Lost

You Saved My Soul

And I Just Want To Thank You

And I Just Want To Praise You

Within My Heart, I Just Want To Love You

Within My Soul

I Just Want To Sing A New Song

To You

The Picture's Changing, I'm Rearranging

The Way I Look At You

Things I Used To Say

The Thoughts Of Everyday

Everything's Changing

Something's Happening Inside Of Me

Something Good, I Feel So Free

Something's Coming Over Me

Couldn't Be Just Me

It's You

It's You

It's You That Makes Me Feel The Way I Do

I Thank You, Lord, I Praise You, Lord

With All My Heart, I Love You, Lord

I Thank You, Lord, I Praise You, Lord

With All My Heart, I Love You, Lord

It's You, It's You\\

JESUS, I NEED YOU

Lord, I Come Before You

Keeping Nothing From You

Take My Life

Make It Right

Jesus, I Need You

Search My Heart

Test My Mind

Cleanse Me From Within

Create In Me

A Clean Heart

As I Repent

Of My Sins

Burn In Me, Holy Fire

Change Me As I Pray

Make Me New

That I May Know

Your Will For Me Today

As I Bow Before You Now

Resting In Your Grace

Fill Me With The Holy Ghost

As I Seek Your Face

Send Me, Lord

Into The World

And Bring Them To The Cross

Put Your Heart And Mind

In Me

To Seek And Save The Lost\\

KNOWING YOU

Lord, I Thank You For Your Mercy

I Thank You For Your Grace

And I Thank You, Holy Spirit

As I Humbly Take My Place

Abiding In The Shadow Of Your Wings

You Keep Me Safe

And I'm All The Better Now

For Knowing You

Knowing You

Has Made The Difference

In All I Say And Do

Knowing You

Has Made The Difference For Me

Born Again Of The Spirit

The Truth Has Set Me Free

Knowing Where My Help

Comes From

Lord, You're Everything To Me

And As I Speak The Name Of Jesus

By Faith, I Receive

Then Peace Comes Over Me

And I Believe

Knowing You

Has Made The Difference

In All I Say And Do

Knowing You

Has Made The Difference For Me

I Lived My Life In Darkness

Trying Ever So Hard To See

Nothing To Hold On To

In This Life Of Misery

But Then, One Night, I Raised My Hand

Saying Jesus Is My Lord

Then I Heard You Speak

And I Knew You Set Me Free

Knowing You

Has Made The Difference

In All I Say And Do

Knowing You

Has Made The Difference

For Me\\

LET ME LIVE FOR YOU

Let Me Live For You

Let Me Do Your Will

Let Me Speak Of Your Love Forever

Let Me Know I Am Yours

Let Me Stay On The Course

That You Have Set In Place For Me

To Follow

Let Me Live My Life

As A Living Sacrifice

That I May Know The Truth Has Set Me Free

Jesus, I Will Worship You Forever

I Will Lift My Voice In Praise

To Honor You

For You Are Worthy

Of All I Have To Give

Please Take All I Am, Let Me Live

For You

Have Mercy On Me

O God, My God

According To Your Lovingkindness

Let The Abundance Of Your Mercy

Cover All Of My Transgressions

Against You, Lord, For I Have Sinned

Purge Me Lord, I Shall Be Clean

Create A Clean Heart Within Me

Let Me Hear The Joy And Gladness

From Your Throne

Jesus, I Will Worship You Forever

I Will Lift My Voice In Praise

To Honor You

For You Are Worthy

Of All I Have To Give

Please Take All I Am, Let Me Live

For You\\

MY REFUGE

My Soul, Wait Silently On God Alone

My Soul, Wait Silently On God Alone

My Expectation Is From Him

He's The Rock Of My Salvation

My Defense, And I Shall Not Be Moved

For In God Is My Salvation

He's My Glory And My Strength

He's My Refuge And I'll Always Trust In Him

O God, You Are My God

Early Will I Seek You

In The Shadow Of Your Wings Will I Sing

In A Dry And Thirsty Land

Where There Is No Water

My Soul Thirsts; My Flesh Longs For You

Trust In Him At All Times

Pour Out Your Heart Before Him

God Is A Refuge For Us

Trust In Him At All Times

Pour Out Your Heart Before Him

God Is A Refuge For Us\\

THE SOUND OF HEAVEN

This Is The Sound

Of Heaven

This Is The Sound Of Change

This Is The Sound

Of Worship

This Is The Sound Of Praise

This Is The Sound

Of Healing

And The Forgiveness Of Our Sins

This Is The Sound

Of Freedom

Lift Up Your Voices, And Sing

I Will Worship You

And Glorify Your Name

Lord, Jesus, Since I Met You

My Life Has Never Been The Same

Lord, I Worship You

And Glorify Your Name

Lord, I Worship You

And Magnify Your Name

Lord, I Worship You,

Hallowed Be Your Name

Lord, Jesus, Because Of You

I Am Saved

Here I Am, Lord, Send Me

Here I Am, Lord, Use Me

Open The Heavens, Lord

And Let Us See

Your Glory, Lord, And Your Majesty

This Is The Sound Of Heaven

Lift Up Your Voices, And Sing

The Sound Of Heaven\\

THERE'S SOMETHING IN THE AIR

There's Something In The Air That Changes

When God Is In The House

Something Beautiful, Invisible, And Powerful

There's Something In The Air All Around Me

And Suddenly I See

That We Are All In One Accord

Worshiping The King

And Then I Know

That We Are The Children Of God

Sometimes I Can See It

Sometimes I Can Feel It

The Holy Ghost Is Moving

Through The Crowd

There's Something In Our Worship

That Shows Who We Really Are

As We Bring The Sacrifice Of Praise To Him

Born Of The Spirit, Justified By Faith

We Have Peace With God

Through Jesus Christ Our Lord

And We Have Come Into This Grace

And This Is Where We Stand

We Rejoice In The Hope Of The Glory

Of God

Delivered From The Darkness

And Walking In The Light

We Have A Friend In Jesus

He Has Given Us New Life

By His Stripes We Are Healed

By His Spirit We Are Sealed

Nothing Shall Separate Us From His Love

And Then I Know

That We Are The Children Of God\\

THIS HOLY PLACE

We Have Come Into This Holy Place

To Bow Before You, Lord

We Have Come To Worship And Bow Down

For You Are Worthy, Lord

We Have Come In Spirit And In Truth

To Worship You, Lord

We Have Come To Praise Your Holy Name

And Give You Glory, Lord

Oh, We Give You Glory, Lord

We Have Come Into This Holy Place

To Sing Your Praises, Lord

We Have Come To Lift Up Holy Hands

For You Are Worthy, Lord

We Have Come In Spirit And In Truth

To Worship You, Lord

We Have Come To Praise Your Holy Name

And Give You Glory, Lord\\

TIME SPENT

Jesus, Jesus, Jesus, My Savior Jesus

Holy Lamb Of God, You Are, You Are

You Alone Are Worthy. Jesus, You Are Holy

Precious Lamb Of God, You Are, You Are

Time Spent, Seeking The Truth

The Meaning Of Life With You, With You

Time Spent, Worshiping You

I Fall On My Knees Again, Again

Search My Heart, Cleanse My Soul

Renew My Mind, And Make Me Whole Again

That I May Worship You, Jesus

In Spirit And In Truth, In Truth

I Will Remember, Remember The Day

You Came Into My Life To Stay

Holy Spirit, Your Grace Is All I Need

Yesterday, And Today, And Forever, Forever

Time Spent, Thinking Of You

Making The Most Of Time Spent With You

Time Spent, Worshiping You

I Fall On My Knees Again, Again\\

UNTIL I'VE GOT NOTHING LEFT

Until I've Got Nothing Left

I'll Give What I Have

Until I've Got Nothing Left

I'll Do All I Can Do

Until I've Got Nothing Left

I'll Take The Message Of The Cross

And The Healing Power

Of The Love Of God

To Seek And Save The Lost

Until I've Got Nothing Left

No Place To Lay My Head

Until I've Got Nothing Left

No Place To Rest

No Place To Call My Home

Until I've Got Nothing Left

And All My Things Are Gone

I'll Live My Life For You

Until I've Got Nothing Left

So Now, All I Have

Is What You See

Lord I Give You Me

Search My Heart

And Test My Mind

And Purge Me

From The Sin You Find

Jesus, I Surrender.

Jesus, I Give Up

Search My Heart

And Test My Mind

And Purge Me

From The Sin You Find

Lose Them In The Sea

Of Forgetfulness

Until I've Got Nothing Left

Walk In The Light, As I Am In The Light

Have Fellowship With Your Friends In Me

And You Shall Have Abundant Life

I Will Never Leave You, My Spirit Is In You

I Bled For You, I Died For You

I Rose Up From The Grave For You

I Love You, I Love You

I Love You, I Love You

Until I've Got Nothing Left

I'll Take The Message Of The Cross

And The Healing Power Of The Love Of God

To Seek And Save The Lost

Until I've Got Nothing Left \\

WORSHIP SONG

There Is None, Lord

Compared To You

Only You Could Change My Life

And Make It New

And In My Heart, Lord

For You, I Long

To Walk With You And Sing

This Worship Song

No More Darkness In My Soul

The Coal Touched My Lips

And Made Me Whole

You Set Me Free

And I Am Free

To Worship You For All Eternity

You Are Worthy

Of All My Praise

You Are Jesus

Name Above All Names

You Are Holy; The Way, The Truth, The Life

I Will Walk With You Forever In The Light

Hallelujah To The Lamb

All Honor, And Power, And Glory

Be Unto The King

And Like A River

Lord, Your Spirit Flows

Throughout The Congregation

As We Sing

No More Darkness In My Soul

The Coal Touched My Lips

And Made Me Whole

You Set Me Free, And I Am Free

To Worship You For All Eternity\\

YOU ARE HOLY

You Are Holy, And Still, You Love Me

I'm Not Worthy Of The Cross

You Gave Your Life For Me

Laid Down Your Rights For Me

And The Day You Rose Again

You Set Me Free

I Will Follow You To The Ends Of The Earth

And By Your Spirit, You Will Lead

When The Healing Comes

Like The Morning Sun

I Will Lift My Hands To You And I Will Sing

You Are Holy, And Still, You Love Me

I'm Not Worthy Of The Cross

You Gave Your Life For Me

Laid Down Your Rights For Me

And The Day You Rose Again

You Set Me Free\\

YOU ARE MY LORD

Lord, You Know I Wasn't Looking

When You Called Out My Name

And When I Turned To You

You Said, Follow Me

Everything That Came Before

Didn't Matter Anymore

I Stopped All That I Was Doing

To Follow You

Lord, Jesus, You Know My Heart

You Had To Know My Sin

And Yet, You Came Anyway

As My Friend.

And Because Of Your Great Love

The Spirit Came To Me

The Gift That Keeps On Giving

Born Again

You Are My Lord, You Are My Savior

You Are My Friend Forevermore

You Heard My Cry

When I Called Your Name, Jesus

You Rescued Me From All My

Guilt And Shame

You Are My Lord

I Pray Today For The Strength

To Stay Away From The Things

That Make Me Think That I Am In Control,

That I Don't Need A Thing

I Pray Today For The Strength

To Stay Away From The Things

That Make Me Think

That I Don't Need To Surrender

I Pray Today For The Strength

To Stay Away From The Things

That Make Me Think That

I Don't Need You As My Savior

I Pray Today For The Strength

To Stay Away From The Things

That Make Me Think That I Don't Need You

As My Lord

Your Grace For My Sins

Your Mercy For My Pride

Your Word For My Pain

Your Life For Mine

Your Strength When I Am Weak

Your Forgiveness For My Sins

Eternal Life For My Soul

Your Life For Mine

From Glory To Glory

The Image That Is Seen

From Glory To Glory

Is The Image Of My King

From Glory To Glory

The Truth Has Set Me Free

From Glory To Glory, I See

You Are My Lord, You Are My Savior

You Are My Friend Forevermore

You Heard My Cry

When I Called Your Name, Jesus

You Rescued Me

From All My Guilt And Shame

You Are My Lord\\

YOU HAVE MY HEART

Hallelujah To The Savior

Hallelujah To The King

Hallelujah To My Lord And My God

The Creator Of All Things

Hallelujah, To The Lamb That Was Slain

Through His Blood I Am Redeemed

Hallelujah, Lord Jesus

You Have My Heart, Lord, You Have Me

Following You Has Been The Joy Of My Life

All My Darkness Has Faded Into The Light

Nothing Can Separate Me From You

Your Spirit Has Changed Me

And Made Me New

And As I Come Into Your Presence

And Fall Down On My Knees

I Can Feel Your Hand Upon Me

You Are All I Need

And As I Speak The Name Of Jesus

Your Peace Comes Over Me

I Can Only Say, I Love You

You Have My Heart, Lord, You Have Me

And In The Church Of The Great I Am

A Joint Heir With The Prince Of Peace

I'm Alive To Him And Dead To Sin

Was Bound But Now

I'm Free\\

CHAPTER 8: FAITH

8

ABSOLUTELY FAITHFUL

I See The Purpose Of Your Love

The Passion Of Your Grace

The Power Of Your Word And I Know

All My Sins Have Been Forgiven

And This Life I Have Today

Truly Testifies To All That You Are God

I'm So Amazed By Your Love

And You're Mercy And Your Grace

I Look Forward To The Day

When I Will Meet You Face To Face

You Are Absolutely Faithful

You Are Absolutely Powerful

You Are Absolutely Everything I Need

You Are Absolutely Amazing

You Are Absolutely Wonderful

And I Absolutely Give My Life To You

And I Know, Yes, I Know

You Are Lord Of My Life

And I Know, Yes, I Know

That You Are God

With All Of My Heart, With All Of My Soul

With All Of My Strength

With All Of My Mind

With All Of My Heart, With All Of My Soul

With All Of My Strength

Lord, I Worship You

With All Power, You Have Given Me

The Gifts And All Authority

To Speak The Name Of Jesus

With Conviction In My Soul

Lord, You Brought Me Out Of Sin

And I Am Born Again

Through The Blood Of Your Own Son

Who Has Come To Set Me Free

I'm So Amazed By Your Love

And Your Mercy And Your Grace

I Look Forward To The Day

When I Will Meet You Face To Face

You Are Absolutely Forgiving

You Are Absolutely Merciful

And You Absolutely Take Me As I Am

You Are Absolutely Holy

You Have Absolutely Changed Me

You Are Absolutely All That I Desire

And I Know, Yes, I Know

You Are Lord Of My Life

And I Know, Yes, I Know That You Are
God\\

COMIN' ON STRONG

Comin' On Strong, Oh yeah

It's Comin' On Strong

It's Comin' On Strong To Set Me Free

Lord, I Wanna Thank You

For The Truth That Sets Me Free

It's Comin' On Strong To Set Me Free

Lord, I Wanna Thank You

For The Blood You Shed For Me

It's Comin' On Strong To Set Me Free

Lord, I Wanna Thank You

For The Love You Have For Me

It's Comin' On Strong To Set Me Free\\

GOTTA REASON TO BELIEVE

Gotta Reason To Believe

That God Became A Man

Born In A Manger

Down In Bethlehem

Gotta Reason To Believe

That Jesus Is The Son Of God

The Son Of Man, The Great I Am

And The Angels Sang

Glory To God In The Highest

Peace On Earth

Goodwill To All Men

I Know He Took My Place

On The Cross

And I Know That He's Coming Again

Gotta Reason To Believe

That All My Sins Are Gone

Nailed To A Cross

Outside Jerusalem

Gotta Reason To Believe

I Can Come Before The Throne

Ask Anything

Cause Jesus Loves Me, This I Know

Gotta Reason To Believe

That I've Been Born Again

Since I Met Jesus

My Life Has Never Been The Same

Gotta Reason To Believe

I've Been Redeemed By The Blood

The Blood Of The Lamb, The Great I Am

And The Angels Sang

Glory To God In The Highest

Peace On Earth, Goodwill To All Men

I Know He Took My Place On The Cross

And I Know That He's Coming Again\\

I FEEL THE POWER

I Feel The Power .Of The Holy Spirit

Comin' Up Inside Of Me

I Feel The Power Of The Holy Spirit

Comin' On Strong To Set Me Free

I Feel It In My Feet

Startin' To Dance A Little Bit More

I Feel It In My Knees

Startin' To Jump And Shout

And Praise The Lord

My Hands Are Liftin' Up

Cause He's Fillin' Up My Cup

I Feel The Holy Spirit

Comin' Up In Me

I Know It In My Mind

Thinkin' About Him All The Time

I Feel It In My Soul

My Name Is On That Holy Roll

You Can See It On My Face

Cause God Is In This Place

I Feel The Holy Spirit Comin' Up In Me

I'm Giving Up My Life

As A Living Sacrifice

I Count It All As Loss

Cause I've Taken Up My Cross

I'm Walking In The Light

Cause He Is In The Light

I Feel The Holy Spirit

Comin' Up In Me

Come, Holy Spirit, Come Up In Me

Let There Be Revival

Set Me Free\\

I'M GIVIN' IT UP

I'm Givin' It Up, I'm Givin' It Up

Just Sayin', If I Got It

And It Didn't Come From God

I'm Givin' It Up

When The Doctor Says This Is It

There's Nothing We Can Do

You Can't Be Fixed

I Say, Doctor, I Don't Know About You

But I Believe In Jesus

And I Know That His Word Is True

I'm Givin' Up Sickness, I'm Givin' Up Pain

I'm Givin' It Up, You Know I Am

If They Say I'm Dying, I Will Live Again

Just Sayin', If I Got It

And It Didn't Come From God

I'm Givin' It Up

When Temptation Gets A Bead On Me

And Says, Go Ahead And Sin

And See How Good It Will Be

I Say, Wait, I Don't Know About You

But I Believe In Jesus

And I Know That His Word Is True

I Am Forgiven, He Delivered Me

I Was Bound In Sin And Jesus Set Me Free

Even When I Mess Up, Jesus Picks Me Up

Just Sayin', If I Got It

And It Didn't Come From God

I'm Givin' It Up

I Say, You, You've Got The Faith

So Speak Unto Your Mountain

And The Mountain's Gotta Move

And You Say, Jesus, I Believe It's True

And I'm Speaking To The Mountain

And The Mountain's Gonna Move

I'm Givin' Up Doubt, I'm Givin' Up Fear

I'm Givin' It Up, Got No Use For It Here

I've Got The Spirit In Jesus Name

Just Sayin', If I Got It

And It Didn't Come From God

I'm Givin' It Up

And When Demons Try To Pull Me In

I Say, Hold On Now, I'm Born Again

I Say, Devil, I Got No Place For You

I Believe In Jesus And I Know

That His Word Is True

I'm Givin' Up Sorrow, I'm Givin' Up Shame

I'm Givin' It Up, You Know I Am

I've Got The Faith In Jesus Name

Just Sayin', If I Got It

And It Didn't Come From God

I'm Givin' It Up\\

IN THE DAY OF TROUBLE

The Lord Is My Light

And My Salvation

Whom Shall I Fear

The Lord Is The Stronghold

Of My Life

Of Whom Shall I Be Afraid

When Evil Men

Advance Against Me

To Slander Me

And Do Me Harm

When My Enemies

And Foes Attack Me

They Will Stumble

And They Will Fall

Though An Army Besiege Me

My Heart Will Not Fear

Though War Break Out Against Me

I Will Have No Fear

One Thing I Ask Of The Lord

And This Is What I Seek

That I May Dwell In His House

Forever

For In The Day Of Trouble

He Will Keep Me Safe

He Will Hide Me In The Shelter

Of His House

And Set Me High Upon A Rock

Then My Head Will Be Exalted

I Will Sing

And Make Music To The Lord\\

IN THE SPIRIT

In The Spirit Of The Lord

I Found Joy

That Makes Me Strong

In The Spirit Of The Lord

I Found Peace

For My Troubled Soul

In The Spirit Of The Lord

I Found Truth

That Sets Me Free

In The Spirit Of The Lord

I Found Love

Beyond Compare

What Once Was

Is Not The Same

Cause In The Spirit

I Have Changed

Crucified With Christ

At Calvary

I'm Born Again, I Am

I've Been Set Free

The Fear Is Gone

He Set Me Free

The Fear Is Gone

When Jesus Sets You Free

You're Free Indeed

I Guarantee, You're Free Indeed

Nothing Can Separate Me

From His Power, His Love, His Grace

The Fear Is Gone\\

JUST ONE THING

Standing On The Threshold

Of A Faith That Moves Mountains

I Humbly Bow Before The Mighty Throne

I've Come To Know The Father

Through The Mercy Of The Son

And In The Name Of Jesus Christ

I Boldly Come

I Believe In The Father

I Found Him Through The Son

I Believe The Holy Spirit Is In Me

And We Are One

I Believe That I'm Accepted

As A Child Of The King

I Believe It All Comes Down

To Just One Thing

I Believe That Jesus Died

And That He Rose Up From The Dead

I Believe That I'm Forgiven

By The Blood That Jesus Shed

I Believe That I Can Do All Things

Through Christ Who Strengthens Me

I Believe The Truth Has Set Me Free

Just One Thing

Has Brought Me To This Place

Just One Thing

Helps Me Receive This Grace

Just One Thing

That Opens Up The Door

To Let Him In

I Take Up My Cross And Follow Him\\

JUST WANT TO SEE

I Am Signed, Sealed, Delivered

By The Blood Of The Lamb

I Am Loved And I'm Forgiven

That's Who I Am

Filled With The Holy Ghost And Fire

I've Been Given My Heart's Desire

I Have An Answer To The Question

When You Ask, What Would Jesus Do

Just Want To See What Jesus Sees

Just Want To Hear What Jesus Hears

Just Want To Speak The Way Jesus Speaks

Just Want To Be All He Says That I Am

You Gave Me Your Faith

You Gave Me Your Hope

You Gave Me Your Love, Your Only Son

You Gave Me Your Peace

You Gave Me Your Joy

You Gave Me Your Word, I Do Believe

You Showed Me The Way

You Showed Me The Truth

You Showed Me The Life

I Live In You

You Gave Me Your Power

You Gave Me Your Plan

You Gave Me Your Grace

And This Is Who I Am

I Am Signed, Sealed, Delivered

By The Blood Of The Lamb

I Am Loved And I'm Forgiven

That's Who I Am

Filled With The Holy Ghost And Fire

I've Been Given My Heart's Desire

I Have An Answer To The Question

When You Ask, What Would Jesus Do

Jesus Loves Me, This I Know

For The Bible Tells Me So

Little Ones To Him Belong

We Are Weak But He Is Strong

Yes, Jesus Loves Me, This I Know

Yes, Jesus Loves Me, This I Know\\

LIVING BY FAITH

Sometimes When I Pray

I Know Just What To Say

I Know I'll See The Answer

By His Word I Have The Faith

God Knows That I Believe

And It's By Faith That I Receive

In Him I Live And Move

I'm Living By Faith

Living By Faith In God Alone

Has Never Been About Me

He's The Strength When I Am Weak

And He Helps My Unbelief

Living By Faith That Jesus Set Me Free

When He Died At Calvary

In Him I Live And Move

I'm Living By Faith

So When I Come To Pray

I Know What To Expect

For Whenever Two Come In His Name

He'll Take Care Of The Rest

I'm Standing On The Promise

Of The One Who Took My Place

In Him I Live And Move

I'm Living By Faith\\

LIVING FOR JESUS

Living For Jesus

It's The Only Thing I Know

Living For Jesus

It's The Only Way To Go

If You're Looking For The Answers

To The Questions Of This Life

Living For Jesus

Is The Only Way

That You Will Get It Right

Living For Jesus

The Creator Of All Things

Living For Jesus

I Shall Ever Follow Him

Living For Jesus

By His Word I'm Born Again

Living For Jesus

I'm Taking Up My Cross

I'm Dead To Sin And Alive In Him

All My Sins Are Gone

Living For Jesus

I Am Saved By Grace Through Faith

In The Name Above All Names

Let All The Earth Proclaim

Hallelujah

He's The Creator Of All Things

Hallelujah

I Shall Ever Follow Him

Hallelujah

By His Word I'm Born Again

Hallelujah

I'm Living For Him\\

MORE THAN ENOUGH

With Ears To Hear, We Shall Draw Near

And Understand The Son Of Man

We Shall Have Faith, We Shall Believe

That Jesus Is More Than Enough

It's Not Enough, For Us

To Say That We Believe

It's Not Enough, For Us

To Listen And Agree

These Ears Don't Understand

So Goes The Mind Of Man

Without The Spirit Of God

It's Not Enough

It's Not Enough, For Us

To Live Without The Savior

It's Not Enough, For Us

To Make It On Our Own

It's Not Enough To Say

I Think, Therefore I Am

Without The Spirit Of God

It's Not Enough, It's Not Enough

With Ears To Hear, We Shall Draw Near

And Understand The Son Of Man

We Shall Have Faith, We Shall Believe

That Jesus Is More Than Enough

More Than Enough, For Us

To Call On Jesus Name

More Than Enough, For Us

To Believe That Our God Reigns

To Surrender And Be Filled

With The Spirit Of The Lord

In Jesus Name, It's More Than Enough

More Than Enough, For Us

To Be In The Kingdom

More Than Enough, For Us

Joint Heirs With Christ, The King

More Than Enough, For Us

To Hear The Holy Spirit

He Speaks, And It's More Than Enough

More Than Enough

With Ears To Hear, We Shall Draw Near

And Understand The Son Of Man

We Shall Have Faith, We Shall Believe

That Jesus Is More Than Enough\\

MY DEAREST COUNTRY

They Were Searching For A Place

A Place Where They Could Pray

Not The Prayers They Had Been Given

But Of Thanksgiving And Praise

Unto God In Jesus Name

They Followed Their Desire

To Speak The Name Of Jesus

And Be Free

They Thought They Found A Home

So They Moved Their Families There

But Time Would Tell, And Living There

Would Be More Than They Could Bear

So They Sailed Upon The Mayflower

To That Land Across The Sea

To Speak The Name Of Jesus

And Be Free

Thank You, Lord, For The Work Of Calvary

Where The Way To Heaven

Was Opened There For Me

Thank You, Jesus

My Soul Cry's Out To Thee

From Place To Place, Toward Heaven

My Dearest Country

Plymouth Rock Was Cold And Dry

And Many Lost Their Lives

But The Natives Soon Became Their Friends

And Helped Them To Survive

And As The Seeds Produced Their Harvest

They Gathered To Give Thanks

For In The Name Of Jesus

They Were Free

Such A Journey We Have Chosen

To Serve Our Lord And King

Such Great Hardships Undertaken

But We Are Born Again

And Though We Search For Peace On Earth

We Know Where We Shall End

From Place To Place, To Heaven

My Dearest Country\\

ONE NATION UNDER GOD

The Words That I Bring You Today

For Such A Time As This

Must Be Heard And Taken As Your Own

For The Greatest Men That Ever Lived

Were Men After God's Own Heart

And They Founded This Great Nation

Under God

To The Character Of Patriot

It Should Be Our Highest Glory

To Add The More Distinguished Name

Of Christian

God Who Gave Us Life

Gave Us Liberty Secured

Through Our Conviction That These Are

The Gifts Of God

No Man Shall Ever Take From Us

The Rights Which Heaven Gave

Steadfastly, We Depend Upon Our God

Trusting Not In The Arm Of Flesh

When Our Cause Is Just And Pure

We Need Not Fear; In Christ We Shall Prevail

The Gospel Of Jesus Christ Prescribes

The Wisest Rule For What We Do

In Every Situation Of Our Life

I've Formed And Settled My Belief

To The Doctrines Of The God Who Speaks

The Word, My Lord And Savior, Jesus Christ

Under God Is Where We Stand

Here With Christ At God's Right Hand

Under God Is Where We Stay

Under God Is Where We Pray

Under God We Have The Strength Of One

The Creator Of All Things

We Are One Nation Under God\\

POWER WALKING

I Was Walking Down The Hall

Of The Pediatric Ward

Pushing My Equipment

Looking For The Door

Found The Number On The Room

Where I Was Called To Be

'Cause I'm The One You Call

When There's Something That You Need

I'm Power Walking, This Is What I Do

Got My Finger On The Pulse

Of The Mighty Holy Ghost

I'm Power Walking, I'm Answering The Call

The Lord Needs Me To Do It, And I Can

'Cause I'm Power Walking

Took A Step Into The Room

Stepped Right Back Out Again

Moved By The Spirit

His Presence Filled The Air

So Now I Knew When I Went In

My Mission Here Was Clear

This Child Needed Help

And God Wants Me Here

I Said, Son, Do You Know Jesus?

And He Said, Yes Sir, I Do

I Said, Jesus Wants To Make You Well

So I'm Here To Pray With You

So I Prayed A Simple Prayer

It's All I Had To Do

He Was Healed In Jesus Name!

I Know This To Be True

Yesterday He Was Dying

Today He's Going Home

But There's More To The Story

There's More You Need To Know

Later, That Same Hour

God Heard Me As I Kneeled

And In A Week The Beds Were Empty

All The Children Had Been Healed

I'm Power Walking\\

ROLL THAT STONE AWAY

They Placed Him In The Tomb And Said

Don't Roll That Stone Away

'Cause He Was Crucified And Died

So Don't Roll That Stone Away

No Matter What You See Or Hear

Don't Roll That Stone Away

But Three Days Later Jesus Rose

And The Stone Was Rolled Away

Roll That Stone Away

Start Walking In The Light

Jesus Said, I Am The Resurrection

And The Life

Roll That Stone Away

'Cause This Is A New Day

Believe It, Receive It, Let's Roll That Stone

Roll That Stone Away

Start Walking In The Light

Jesus Said, I Came

That You Might Have Abundant Life

Roll That Stone Away

'Cause This Is A New Day

Believe It, Receive It, Let's Roll

When Darkness Overtakes You

Roll That Stone Away

When The Devil's Got A Hold On You

Roll That Stone Away

When Sickness Tries To Take Your Life

Roll That Stone Away

When Addiction Starts To Pull You Down

Roll That Stone Away

When You Think That You're

Not Good Enough

Roll That Stone Away

When Your Life Is All About Your Stuff

Roll That Stone Away

When Death Is Knocking At Your Door

Roll That Stone Away

Jesus Came To Give You Life

So Roll That Stone Away

When Desperation Takes Its Toll

Roll That Stone Away

With Eyes Wide Open, See The Goal

And Roll That Stone Away

If You Think That You're Not Strong Enough

To Roll That Stone Away

In Your Weakness, He Is Strong

So Roll That Stone Away

Roll That Stone Away

Start Walking In The Light

Jesus Said, I Am The Resurrection

And The Life

Roll That Stone Away

'Cause This Is A New Day

Believe It, Receive It, Let's Roll That Stone

Roll That Stone Away

Start Walking In The Light

Jesus Said, I Came

That You Might Have Abundant Life

Roll That Stone Away

'Cause This Is A New Day

Believe It, Receive It, Let's Roll\\

SON OF GOD

I Live My Life By The Faith

Of The Son Of God

I Pray To The Father In The Name

Of The Son Of God

Yes, I Am Crucified

With The Son Of God

And Yet, I Live By The Faith

Of The Son Of God

He Believed In The Father

As He Died On The Cross

And His Only Desire

Was To Save The Lost

Son Of God

He Believed In The Father

And He Rose From The Grave

And His Only Desire

Was For Us To Be Saved

Son Of God

God Will Always Do For You

What Only He Can

Do Through You

Son Of God

Greater Is He, Greater Is He

Greater Is He In Me

Greater Is He, Greater Is He

Than He Who Is In

The World

I Live My Life By The Faith

Of The Son Of God

I Pray To The Father

In The Name Of The Son Of God

Yes, I Am Crucified

With The Son Of God

And Yet, I Live By The Faith

Of The Son Of God

Son Of God!\\

TIME TO GET UP

All His Life Has Been Spent Right Here

Begging Every Day

Been Lame Since The Day He Was Born

Didn't Know Any Other Way

Right There, At The Gate Called Beautiful

Full Of Sorrow, Full Of Shame

Hoping Against Hope

That He'd Get Some Help Today

Trying To Make It On His Own

Just Trying To Survive

Just Another Day Gone By

Just Another Night

He Never Looked Them In The Eye

But He Was Always There

Just Wanted Them To Know The Truth

Just Wanted Them To Care

I Remember When We Went To Him

And Looked Into His Eyes

The Emptiness Inside

Was Like The Darkest Night

He Thought We Came With Silver And Gold

But We Came With New Life

Peter Took His Hand And Said

Rise Up, In The Name Of Jesus Christ

And He Got Up, And He Walked

For The First Time In His Life

He Got Up, He Was So Happy

Leaping And Dancing

And Praising The Lord

He Got Up And Now Everyone Could See

That God Had Worked A Miracle

And It Was Done In The Name Of Jesus

Do You Remember

When Jesus Found You In Your Sin

And When You Believed

You Were Born Again

The Power Is Within You Now

The Word Abides Within

The Promises Are Yours By Faith

By Faith In Jesus Christ

So Now, Get Up, And Get Moving

By His Stripes, Receive Your Healing

Yes, Get Up, He Has Delivered You

From The Darkness Into The Light

Now, Get Up, And Tell Everyone You See

That God Has Worked A Miracle

And It Was Done In The Name

It Was Done In The Name

It Is Finished In The Name Of Jesus\\

WE'VE GOT THE DEVIL ON THE RUN

Jesus Breathed, I Received

The Holy Spirit Is In Me

The Fear Is Gone And I Am Free

The Devil Lost His Hold On Me

The Word Of God Is On My Mind

Changing Who I Am Inside

Born Again Of The Spirit

Speaking Out So All Can Hear It

Jesus Is The Lord Of My Life

We've Got The Devil On The Run

The Gates Of Hell Shall Not Prevail

Against The Kingdom Of God

No Weapon Formed Against Us

Will Succeed

We've Not Been Given A Spirit Of Fear

But Of Power And Love

And Ears To Hear

Resisting Now, The Devil, He Will Flee

Crucified With Christ, We Are

And Risen From The Dead

Justified By Faith, We're Spirit Led

Standing As A Shining Light

For All The World To See

Jesus Has Become Our Victory

We've Got The Devil On The Run\\

WHEN WE SING HALLELUJAH

Hallelujah, Hallelujah, Hallelujah

Holy, Holy Is The King

When We Sing Hallelujah

Do You Know What It Means

When We Speak Of The One

Who Rose Again

Do You Know Why He Died

Do You Know That As He Hung

Upon The Cross

The Blood He Shed Was For You

Name Above All Names

Do You Know Who He Was

When We Speak Of The King Of Kings

Do You Know Who We Mean

Crucified To Forgive Us Our Sins

And For Us, He'll Come Again

There Is No Greater Love Than This

He Laid Down His Life For You

Son Of God; Son Of Man

Jesus, Our Savior; The Lamb

When We Sing Hallelujah

Holy, Holy Is The King

When We Praise The Name Of Jesus

You Can Hear The Angels Sing

Hallelujah, Hallelujah, Hallelujah

Holy, Holy Is The King

When We Sing Hallelujah

Do You Worship The King

Do You Lift Your Hands

And Praise His Holy Name

Do You Know That Our God Reigns

Do You Know, Have You Heard

The Voice Of God

Does His Spirit Dwell In You

Do You Know, You Are Saved By Grace

Through Faith

Not By Anything You Do

When We Sing Hallelujah

Holy, Holy Is The King

When We Praise The Name Of Jesus

You Can Hear The Angels Sing

Hallelujah, Holy, Holy Is The King\\

CHAPTER 9: HOPE

9

AS THE ROCKS BEGIN TO FLY

As The Rocks Begin To Fly

I Look Up, My Face To The Sky

Nowhere To Go, Nowhere To Run

But I Know From Where My Help

Comes From

And Then, As They Cast

Their Judgments Upon Me

I Remember I Have The Victory

Jesus Is All I Need; The Truth Is In Me

And I Am Free, I Am Free

Do You See What I See

Can You See The Heavens Open Wide

Do You Know What I Know

Do You See The Angels At My Side

Do You See What I See

Do You See The Savior Standing Strong

Do You Hear What I Hear

They're Singing My Song

Rejoice, Rejoice, Again I Say, Rejoice

Holy, Holy, Is The Lord, Almighty, Rejoice\\

CAN'T STOP THE TEARS

Seems Like Moments Ago

I Felt So Weak

Was On My Knees

But I Couldn't Speak

Wasting Away

Day After Day

Still Wondering How I Got Here

As I Watched My Life Slip Away

Can't Stop The Tears

Of All The Years

Can't Stop The Tears Of Pain And Sadness

Of My Dark And Broken Soul

Can't Stop The Tears

Can't Stop The Fear

Of Never Having The Chance Again

To Make Things Right

Where Do I Go?

What Should I Do?

These Are The Questions

I Brought To You

Have No Fear, You Say,

I'll Pray With You

Now, Come And Talk To Jesus

And Tell Him What's On Your Mind

You Told Me Jesus Loves Me

And Has Forgiven All My Sins

And In My Heart, I Believed

And I Was Born Again

Peace Came Over Me

Unlike Anything I've Known

And That Day, I Met Jesus

And I'll Never Be Alone

Can't Stop The Tears

The Day Had Finally Come

Can't Stop The Tears

My New Life Has Begun

Can't Stop The Tears

More Love Than I Have Ever Known

Can't Stop The Tears

And I Want Everyone To Know

He Opened My Eyes

To The Darkness Of My Soul

And His Light Shines In The Darkness

And Makes Me Whole

One Step Below The Bottom

Where I Thought That I Would Die

That's Where Jesus Found Me

And It Still Makes Me Cry

Can't Stop The Tears

The Day Had Finally Come

Can't Stop The Tears

My New Life Has Begun

Can't Stop The Tears

More Love Than I Have Ever Known

Can't Stop The Tears

And I Want Everyone To Know\\

ETERNITY

Will My Faith Always Be Threatened

By The Questions Of This Life

Or Can I Really Keep My Eyes

Fixed On Jesus Christ

Is There Peace That I Can Find Here

A Better Place That I Can Be

Is The Grass Greener On The Other Side

Or Has Jesus Set Me Free

He Set Me Free, Yes, He Did

I Heard Him Knocking On The Door

I Heard His Voice, I Heard Him Say

"You Can Live Forevermore"

The Holy Spirit Came When I Proclaimed

That Jesus Is My Lord

He Set Me Free

And Now I Live For All Eternity

Eternity, I'm No Longer Of This World

Eternity, I'm A Child Of The King

Eternity, Even Now Abides In Me

The Word Of Truth For All Eternity

I Am Free Now From Depression

Anxiety And Pain

I Am Healed Of All Infirmity

By The Power Of Jesus Name

And The Word Gives Me What I Can't See

That Helps Me To Believe

God's Grace Is Sufficient

God's Grace Is All I Need

Eternity, I Am Hidden With Christ In God

Victory, O'er The Power Of Death And Sin

Born Again, In The Spirit I Am Free

To Live My Life For All Eternity\\

EXCEPT FOR YOU

If I Could Go Back And Change Everything

I Would If I Could

Change Everything That I've Done

I Would Change Everything Except For You

If I Could Go Back

And Somehow Avoid All The Pain

And The Shame That I Carried With Me

I Would Change Everything Except For You

I'm So Amazed By The Difference

You Make In My Life

Every Day As Your Love Overtakes Me

And Changes Everything Except For You

You're The Reason I Laugh

And The Reason I Sing

And I Know That I'm Lost Without You

You Have Changed Everything

Except For You

Not My Will, But Yours Be Done

I Will Drink From This Cup Of New Life

And Overcome

Not My Will, But Yours Be Done

In My Spirit I Know I Am Changed

By The Blood Of The Son

Now I Know All These Things

Work Together For Good

And The Joy Of The Lord

Is My Strength

And It Changes Everything

Except For You

You're The Same Every day

And The Same Every Hour

Your Love Is Amazing

Your Mercy Has Changed Everything

Except For You

Your Forgiveness And Mercy

And Undeserved Love For Me

Is So Amazing To Me

It Has Changed Everything

Except For You

Now Nothing Can Separate Me

From The Love I Have Found

In My Savior, Lord Jesus

It Changed Everything

Except For You

Not My Will, But Yours Be Done

I Will Drink From This Cup

Of New Life

And Overcome

Not My Will, But Yours Be Done

In My Spirit I Know I Am Changed

By The Blood Of The Son\\

FREE TO SERVE

For All Of Those Who Stand

For The Freedoms We Now Have

And For All Of Those Who Fight For Good

And Eradicate The Bad

For All Of Those Who Shed Their Blood

For Truth And Liberty

For All Of Those Who Lost Their Lives

And Gave This Life To Me

I Stand In Your Shadow

Honoring Your Name

I Thank You For Your Sacrifice

Because Of You, My World Has Changed

And Everything That Was

Is Replaced By Something New

A Better, More Abundant Life

Is Here Because Of You

I'm Free To Serve

Nothing In This World Compares

To All You've Given Me

And No One Can Take Away

From All You've Done To Keep Me Free

It's On This Sacred Ground I Walk

In Freedom Everyday

You Secured My Right

Through Your Sacrifice

To Speak My Mind And Pray

Heroes Always Do For Us

What God Has Given Them

They Rise To The Occasion

To Meet The Needs At Hand

And When They Have Succeeded

And Their Work Is Finally Done

History Will Honor Them

For The Victories They Have Won

I Stand In Your Shadow

Honoring Your Name

I Thank You For Your Sacrifice

Because Of You, My World Has Changed

And Everything That Was

Is Replaced By Something New

A Better, More Abundant Life

Is Here Because Of You

I'm Free To Serve

I'm Free To Serve My God

I'm Free To Serve My Fellow Man

In Any Way I Choose

I'm Free To Take A Stand

I'm Free To Speak The Truth

I'm Free To Serve My Country

And It's All Because Of You

Because Of You

I'm Free To Serve\\

HELP ME JESUS

Help Me, Jesus, When Things Aren't Right

And I Don't Know What To Do

Help Me, Jesus, To Remember

That I Can Turn To You

Help Me, Jesus, To Make My Prayers

More Than Prayers Into The Air

Help Me, Jesus, Please Help Me

Help Me, Jesus

Help Me Do The Things I Need To Do

Help Me, Jesus

To Walk And Talk Everyday With You

Help Me, Jesus

And Let Your Glory Shine In Me

That All The World May See

That Jesus Helps Me

Help Me, Jesus, To Always Speak The Truth

When I Know That I Am Right

Help Me, Jesus, To Be Patient

When I Want To Stand And Fight

Help Me, Jesus, To Be At Peace

With Trouble In My Life

Help Me, Jesus, Please Help Me

Help Me, Jesus, Every Day, To Be A Witness

With The Message Of The Cross

Help Me, Jesus, To Never Judge

But Always Show God's Love

Help Me, Jesus, To Walk In Faith

In Spirit And In Truth

Help Me, Jesus, Please Help Me\\

HOW DO I KNOW

If I Believe I'm Headed The Right Way Today

But The Way That I'm Headed Is Wrong

I'm Believing A Lie

But How Do I Know?

If I Believe All The Words That I Speak

Are The Truth

But That Which I Speak Is All Wrong

I'm Believing A Lie

But How Do I Know?

If I Believe That My Life Is All It Can Be

But There's Life Beyond All That I See

I'm Believing A Lie

But How Do I Know?

If Only The Way Had A Voice

And Could Speak

It Could Tell Me Which Way I Should Go

But How Do I Know

If The Way Cannot Speak?

If Only The Truth Had A Voice I Could Hear

It Could Give Me The Words I Should Say

But How Do I Know

If The Truth I Can't Hear?

If Only My Life Had Command

Of My Thoughts

It Could Tell Me Just How I Should Live

But How Do I Know

If Life Has No Words?

Perhaps If The Words Became Flesh

And Could Speak

Then The Way I Should Go Could Be Known

Then I Would Know

If The Words Came To Life!

Perhaps If The Truth Could Speak

To My Soul

So The Words Would Be More Than My Own

Then I Would Know

If The Truth Had A Voice!

Perhaps If I Walked In This Spirit Of Truth

I Would Know I Have Found A Good Life

Then I Would Know

If Life Could Just Speak!

Now, Suppose That All This

Has Already Been Done

And The Path Set Before Me Is Lit

Then I Would Know

Because Then I Could See!

And Suppose, In That Light

A Voice Speaks To My Soul

With The Truth Of What I Should Say

Then I Would Know

Because Then I Could Hear!

And Suppose That This Light

Is The Life That I Seek

And Is Given To All Who Believe

Then I Would Know

Because Then I'd Believe!

Now, The Stories Are True

And The Plan Is Complete

All Because Of A Death On A Cross

How Do I Know?

Because Now I Can See!

Now, His Name Is Jesus, The Messiah

Our God

And His Mission: Restoring The Lost

How Do I Know?

Because Now I Can Hear!

Now, He Suffered And Died

Was For Us Crucified

And Forgave Us For All Of Our Sins

How Do I Know?

Because Now I Believe!

I Am The Way, And The Truth, And The Life

Are The Words Of Our Lord, Jesus Christ

How Do I Know?

Because I Found The Way

And Because He Has Risen

His Words Still Apply

And He's Offering All A New Life!

How Do I Know?

Because I Know The Truth

So, The Way Has A Voice

And The Truth Sets Us Free

And The Life Is A Light For All To See

How Do I Know? Because I Found Life

How Do I Know? Because He Say's So!

Whenever I Pray, He Is Near!\\

I'M A CHILD OF THE KING

Here Again, I Find Myself

In The Presence Of My God

It Seems Just So Unlikely

That He Would Want To Be With Me

And I Look Around As I Hear The Sound

Of Laughter From The King

And He Says. It's So Good To Be With You,

Now Ask Me

Anything

And Then Peace Comes Over Me

And I'm Feeling, Oh, So Free

And I Never Want To Walk Away Again

He Makes Me Feel Like I Belong

I'm In His Family

And I Can Talk To Him About Everything

'Cause I'm A Child

Of The King

Here Again, I Find Myself

At The Mercy Of My King

Jesus Is Here With Me

And The Spirit Brought Me In

And The Father Listens Patiently

As I Bring Him All My Needs

And He Says, I'll Give You Everything

For In You

I See Me

Spending So Much Precious Time

Trying Not To Sin

Sometimes This World Makes Me Forget

That I Am Born Again

Then, In My Ear, The Spirit Says

God Loves You, Now, Begin

And I Rise And Walk In Power

'Cause I'm A Child Of The King\\

IT WILL BE ALL RIGHT

Even When You Don't

Get It Right

Jesus Is The Way

The Truth, The Life

The Alpha And Omega

The Beginning

And The End

Even When You Don't

Get It Right

He's Still Your Friend

It Will Be All Right

He Has You In His Sight

He's Watching Over You

And He Knows Just What To Do

It Will Be All Right

He Came To Give You Life

Just Turn To Him

And It Will Be All Right

Count It All Joy

When You Fall

And Let Patience Have

Its Perfect Work

You Will Hear His Voice

And In Your Heart

You Will Rejoice

Be Still And You Will Find

The Faith To Know

That It Will Be All Right

It Will Be All Right

He Has You In His Sight

He's Watching Over You

And He Knows Just What To Do

It Will Be All Right

He Came To Give You Life

Just Turn To Him

And It Will Be All Right

Do Not Be Afraid

When Things Don't Go Your Way

It Can't Be Fixed By Power Or By Might

By My Spirit, Says The Lord

I Will Redeem The Day

Faith, Hope, And Love Are Here To Stay

And It Will Be All Right\\

I'VE GOT JESUS HERE WITH ME

Been A Long Time Coming

But I Finally Found The Peace

That I've Been Searching For All Of My Life

And It's So, So Much More

Than I Thought That It Would Be

And It Comes From A Deeper Place In Me

I've Got Jesus Here With Me

The Holy Spirit Came

When Jesus Set Me Free

And From Glory To Glory, I Receive

I've Got Jesus Here With Me

Been A Long, Long Road

That I Have Traveled On

And At Times It Wasn't Easy

To Make It Through

But Because I Have A Friend

Who Is The Beginning And The End

I'm Not Worried For My Future Is With Him

Yes, I Know That Jesus Loves Me

I Found A Friend In Him

My Past Is Gone, He's Given Me New Life

And This Life Is More Abundant

Than I Thought That It Would Be

Since He Breathed His Spirit Into Me

I've Got Jesus Here With Me

The Holy Spirit Came

When Jesus Set Me Free

And From Glory To Glory, I Receive

I've Got Jesus Here With Me\\

JUST TO SURVIVE

Tough Times, Stressed Out

Between A Hard Place And A Rock

No Place To Stay, No Place To Go

Invisible, I Walk

A Few Small Coins, A Scrap Of Food

Keeps Me On My Way

Pay My Dues, Ease The Pain

To Walk Another Day

Can You Hear Me? I'm Crying Out!

Can You Help Me? I Can't Help Myself!

Can You See Me? Do You Understand?

You've Given Up On Me

And Now I've Lost My Mind

Just To Survive

Unclean, Unclean!

Is That What You Want To Hear?

Out Of Sight, Out Of Mind

So You'll Never Have To Fear!

Drop Me Off For A Plate Of Food

And A Place To Sleep Tonight

But Morning Comes, Back On The Street

No Dignity In Sight

Can You Hear Me? I'm Crying Out!

Can You Help Me? I Can't Help Myself!

Can You See Me? Do You Understand?

You've Given Up On Me

And Now I've Lost My Mind

Just To Survive

Is There Something I Can Do, I Asked

To Be Who I Used To Be

Is There Someone I Can Talk To

Who Understands My Need?

Maybe I Don't Need, I Said

To Get Back To Who I Was

Maybe I Just Need Someone

To Tell Me.... I Am Loved

Well, There Was Somebody Out There

Who Understood My Plight

There Was Somebody Out There Who
Offered Me New Life

I Found Out Jesus Loves Me, And That He's
Alive And Well

And He Lived And Died And Rose Again

To Deliver Me....From Hell

Can You Hear Me? I Was Crying Out! Can
You Help Me? I Can't Help Myself!

Can You See Me? Do You Understand? The
World's Given Up On Me....

And Now.... My Mind Is Sound

And Grace Abounds

Now, Crucified With Christ

And Yet I Am Alive

And It Means So Much More To Me

Than Just To Survive\\

LET NOT YOUR HEART BE TROUBLED

Let Not Your Heart Be Troubled

If You Believe In God, Believe In Me

In My Father's House Are Many Mansions.

If It Were Not So

I Would Have Let You Know

I Go To Prepare A Place For You

I Will Come Again And Receive You Unto Me

I Go To Prepare A Place For You

That Where I Am, There You Shall Be\\

ONE HOPE

Lord, You Took My Sins

And Nailed Them To The Cross

Lord, I Gladly Give My Life

To You

One Hope, One Love

One Reason To Live

Is All I Need

One Word, One God

One Cause Worth Dying For

One Way, One Truth

My Life Will Never Be The Same

One Life, One Light, One Spirit

One Name Above All Names

Lord, I Will Speak Your Word

To The Ends Of The Earth

And The Disciples

Of All Nations

Will Be Free

And Lord, Into This World

I'll Take The Message Of The Cross

So That Others Will See Jesus

And Believe\\

ONE STEP BELOW THE BOTTOM

I've Been Down At The Bottom

So Alone, So Empty And Blue

It's So Dark At The Bottom

No Where To Go, Don't Know What To Do

What Do You Do When It Gets So Bad

It's Just Not Real Anymore

What Do You Do When The Darkness Comes

And Takes You Like A Storm

I've Been Down At The Bottom

So Alone, So Empty And Blue

It's So Dark At The Bottom

No Where To Go, Don't Know What To Do

When I Can't See Any Way Out

Will Jesus Take Me Through

One Step Below The Bottom

Do I Hang On To What I Have

Or Just Let Go

One Step Below The Bottom

That's Where I Let Go

One Step Below The Bottom

Jesus Met Me There, This I Know

One Step Below The Bottom

I Surrendered My Life Again To Him

One Step Below The Bottom

Now I Go There Every Day To Be With Him

Prayer To My Savior

Prayer To My Lord

Prayer To The Very End

Prayer To Jesus, My Friend

Prayer Saved My Soul

Prayer Made Me Whole

Prayer,

All I Need Is Prayer

One Step Below The Bottom

I Surrender My Life To Him

One Step Below The Bottom

Now I Go There Every Day To Be With Him

Yes, I Go There Every Day

To Speak With Him\\

PUT IT IN THE HANDS OF GOD

Does It Seem Like

Everything Is Going Bad For You

Put It In The Hands Of God

Does It Seem Like Everybody Knows

What's Going On With You, But You

Put It In The Hands Of God

You Can Trust Him To Take It

And Make It Work Out

You Can Trust Him To Know What To Do

You Can Trust That He Will Do

What He Needs To Do

To Make All Things Work Together For You

Does It Seem Like Everybody Knows

What They Think You Should Do

Put It In The Hands Of God

Does It Seem Like You're All Alone

And People Don't Have A Clue

Put It In The Hands Of God

Everything You Want, Everything You Need

Every Open Door, Every Victory

Every Sorrow Gone, Every Shame Dismissed

Every Sin Forgiven, Trouble All Erased

All Your Wrongs Forgotten

Nothing Held Against You

If You Have A Question, Jesus Is The Answer

Put It In The Hands Of God\\

YOU SPEAK THE TRUTH

When It's All That I Can Do

Just To Make It Through The Day

And The Cares Of This Life

Have Got Me Down

When I Need Someone To Hear Me

Someone Who Understands

Someone Who Really Cares

If I'm Alive

When It Comes Down To The End

Still Lookin' For The Answer

And I Don't Think I Can Do This

Anymore

Then You Tell Me I'm Forgiven

You Reach Out And Take My Hand

And I Feel The Love Of God In You

My Friend

You Speak The Truth

And It All Becomes So Clear To Me

You Speak The Truth

And It's All I Need To Hear

You Speak The Truth

And My Spirit Is Set Free Again

And I Know That God Is With Me

And I Know I'm Not Alone

And I Know That Jesus Loves Me

And I Know

You Speak The Truth

When I Find Myself In Trouble

And I Want To Run And Hide

Somehow You Always Find Me

And You Bring Me Back Inside

'Cause In Your Eyes I'm Family

It's A Love I Can't Deny

You Tell Me

I Can Leave My Way Of Life

And Change My Mind

And When I'm Kneeling At The Altar

Asking God To Hear My Prayer

With Your Hand Upon My Head

It's Almost More Than I Can Bear

'Cause I Hear The Holy Spirit Saying

Peace, My Child, Be Still

Just Trust And Obey

Yes, Lord, I Will

When I Lift My Hands To Worship

As The Music Soothes My Soul

Nothing Compares To What I Feel

As The Lyrics Reach Their Goal

'Cause I Know I'm In The Presence

And There Are Angels All Around

Together We Are Lifting

Up Our Voices

To The Lamb

And It's All That I Can Do

Just To Stand Here With You

As We Sing Of His Mercy And His Grace

And As The Power Of This Blessing

Takes Me Beyond Myself

I Understand My Purpose In This Place

Now Jesus Is My Teacher

And The One Who Made Me Whole

He Died And Rose Again To Save My Soul

And The Holy Ghost Has Changed Me

From The Person That I Was

All Because You Preached

The Message Of God's Love

And Now, In Quiet Expectation

I Wait For You To Speak

The Word Of God Is In Your Hands

And This Message Is For Me

Then I See That Look Upon Your Face

And The Fire In Your Eyes

As You Teach Us How To Walk

In The Light

You Speak The Truth And I Am Broken

By God's Spirit In This Place

You Speak The Truth And I Am Humbled

As I Fall Down On My Face

You Speak The Truth

And I'm Delivered

And Forgiven For My Sins

You Speak The Truth

And I Believe

That I'm A Child Of The King

You Speak The Truth\\

CHAPTER 10: LOVE

10

A LOVE LIKE THIS

We Sing Holy, We Sing Holy

We Sing Holy, Holy Is The Lord

Such A Wonderful Feeling

To Be Here With You

Knowing All My Sins Have Been Forgiven

Such A Perfect Peace, I Find In You

A Love Like This Can Only Last Forever

I Am, He Said

The Resurrection And The Life

Believe In Me

And You Shall Walk In The Light

By Grace Are You Saved

Not By Works, But By Faith

Trust In Me

I Made Forever Just For You

We Sing Holy, We Sing Holy

We Sing Holy, Holy Is The Lord

Such A Wonderful Savior

My Lord And My God

Everlasting Father, Counselor To All

Emmanuel, God With Us

King Of Kings, Christ Jesus

The Greatness Of Your Love

Endures Forever

I Lift Up My Hands

And Praise Your Holy Name

Jesus, My Redeemer

Forever Shall You Reign

I Lift Up My Hands

And Praise Your Holy Name

A Love Like This Can Only Last Forever

We Sing Holy, We Sing Holy

We Sing Holy, Holy Is The Lord

A Love Like This Can Only Last Forever\\

BEAUTIFUL BRIDE

As He Looked Upon His Bride

Glowing Bright In The Light Of Love

He Knew That This Moment

Would Last Forever

A Moment Ordained By God

He Knows What This Love Requires

As He Gives Up His Place In Time

To Be Forever With His Beautiful Bride

Was All That Was On His Mind

She'll Never Forget How She Felt

When She Looked Into His Eyes, So True

She Knew He Would Never Give Up

'Till He Captured Her Heart

And She Said, I Do

Beautiful Bride Of Mine

Perfect In Every Way

Beautiful Bride Of Mine

Forever I'll Love You Today

Everything I Am, Everything I Have

Everything I Do Is For You

I Would Lay Down My Life

And Take It Up Again

If It Meant I Could Be Here With You\\

BEYOND THE CROSS

Holy Father

We Stand In Your Presence

As Joint Heirs With Christ, The King

Healed Of All Infirmities, Forgiven Of All Sin

Remembering What Once We Were

And Counting It As Loss

We Thank You, Lord, For This New Life

With You, Beyond The Cross

Beyond The Cross

There Is Nothing In My Past

Beyond The Cross, I Have Everything I Ask

Beyond The Cross

Jesus Christ Has Taken Me

Beyond The Power Of Sin And Death

Christ Has Set Me Free

Beyond The Cross, I Am Forever Changed

Beyond The Cross

Still God Remains The Same

Beyond The Cross, The Captives Are Set Free

As We Proclaim The Name Of Jesus

Beyond The Cross

Committing All I Do

Lord I Put My Trust In You

Knowing That You're With Me

In Everything I Do

I Love You, Lord, With All My Heart,

With All My Mind And All My Soul

Your Holy Spirit Has Lifted Me

To A Place Of Power And Of Love

Beyond The Cross

There Is No Place For Doubt And Fear

In The Fellowship We Have With God\\

CAPTURED BY THE LOVE

Sin Stained My Life

It Stuck To My Soul

Like Sap On A Tree

But There Is A Savior

Who's Blood Cleansed My Soul

He Did This For Me

Born Of The Spirit

Joint Heirs With The Son

Isn't This Me?

Nothing Can Compare

To The Glory Of The Lord

And He Is In Me

I'm Captured By The Love

And Saved By Grace Through Faith

Redeemed By The Blood

Of The One Who Took My Place

Jesus Is The King

Who Came To Rescue Me From Sin

That Had Me Bound But Now I'm Free

Christ Jesus Set Me Free

I'm Captured By The Love

Walking In The Light

I Look Into His Eyes

And He Sees Me

I Open Up My Mouth

And He Gives Me The Words

That Set People Free

Healing Broken Hearts

Bringing Good News To The Poor

That Jesus Is Lord

Thank You For Your Mercy

Thank You For Your Grace

I Couldn't Ask For Any More

I'm Captured By The Love\\

COVER ME (MY FATHER'S CHILD)

Was A Time

When All The Pain In My Life

Was All That I Could See

But Then I Looked Into My Savior's Face

Such Amazing Grace

My Father's Child

You Covered Me, Holy Father

You Covered Me, With Your Great Love

You Covered All My Sins Forever

I Shall Always Be My Father's Child

With These Eyes

I Have Seen The Light Of Life

In All Of Those

Who Have Believed

Covered By The Blood

And Rescued From The Dark

I Truly Am My Father's Child

Cover Me, Oh Lord

Let Me Stay In Your Embrace

As I Speak Of When The Savior Captured Me

I Am Humbled By His Love

Everywhere I Go

My Prayer Shall Always Be,

That You Only See

My Father's Child\\

FAITH, HOPE, AND LOVE

All Of The Things Of This World

Will Pass Away, Pass Away

All The Cares Of My Life

Will Pass Away, Pass Away

All The Pain, Sorrow, And Tears

Will Pass Away, Pass Away

All My Life Long Fears

Will Pass Away, Pass Away

But Faith, Hope, And Love

Are Forever

He Has Delivered Us

From The Power Of Darkness

And Translated Us

Into The Kingdom Of Jesus, His Son

In Whom We Have Redemption

Through Blood,

The Forgiveness Of Sins

He Is The Image Of The Invisible God,

The First Born Over All

For By Him All Things Were Created

Things In Heaven

And Things On The Earth

Everything We See, Everything We Don't

Whether Thrones Or Dominions Or Powers,

All Things Were Created By Him

And For Him

I Know This Faith I Have In God

Will Not Pass Away

And This Hope I Have In Christ

Will Not Pass Away

And This Love I Don't Deserve

Will Not Pass Away

'Cause He Took Away My Sins

When He Passed Away

And I Know He Conquered Death

'Cause He Rose Up From The Grave

And He Made A Place For Me

In Heaven

And Faith, Hope, And Love

Are Forever\\

FALL IN LOVE WITH YOU

I Need To Love You, Lord

With All My Heart

With All My Soul, With All My Mind

I Need To Love You, Lord

Fall In Love With You

I Want To Love You, Lord

With All My Heart

With All My Soul, With All My Mind

I Want To Love You, Lord

Fall In Love With You

Come Taste And See, The Lord Is Good

Come Taste And See

And Know The Lord Is Good

I Love You, Lord With All My Heart

With All My Soul, With All My Mind

I Love You, Lord,

I Fall In Love With You\\

GOD'S LIKE THAT

She Speaks In A Quiet Voice

Just Above A Whisper

They Have To Strain To Hear

That's How She Knows They're Listening

And As She Looks Into Their Eyes

There Is No Compromise

A Mother's Love Knows No Bounds

God's Like That

As He Speaks With A Still Small Voice

That Gives Us Pause

And Makes Us Stop And Listen

God's Like That

As He Opens Our Eyes To See

God's Love Is Without Condition

Oh, She Remembers Well

When They Were In Her Womb

That New Life

That Was Growing Inside

And As She Looks At Them Now

They Really Don't Have A Clue

She Sees A Miracle Before Her Eyes

God's Like That

As He Knew You Before You Were Born

He Was Watching Over You

When You Stretched Those Little Arms

God's Like That

He's Watching You Even Now

He Sees A Miracle Before His Eyes

Somehow A Mother Knows

When Something Isn't Right

She Knows When She Needs To Pray

And For Her Children, She Will Fight

And Even If They Go Astray

She Won't Look The Other Way

She Forgives, She Prays, She Waits

God's Like That

As He Knows Just What We Need

Before We Ask

Even When We Go Astray

He Never Looks Away

God's Like That

And His Love Is Everlasting

He Forgives, He Loves, He Waits

God's Like That

He Brings Good News To The Poor

He Is Setting People Free

And Healing Broken Hearts

God's Like That

Working All Things For Your Good

He Loves You, Jesus Loves You

He's Like That\\

GOD'S LOVE

God's Love Came Down

From Above

When Jesus Became One Of Us

God's Hope, God's Plan

Is That Everyone

Be Born Again

Nothing Can Separate Us

From The Love Of The Father

In Jesus

Nothing Can Change What He's Already

Finished For Us

On The Cross

Nothing I Know Can Compare

To This New Life I Have

In Jesus

If There's One Thing I Know I Can Have,

It's God's Love

God's Love Gives Me Peace

God's Love Gives Me Joy

God's Love Gives Me Wisdom

To Know The Truth That Sets Me Free

No Greater Love, Can We Have

Than To Lay Down Our Lives

For Our Friends

No Greater Love Can Be Found

In All The World

This Love We Have From God

It Never Ends\\

GOOD, GOOD FRIDAY

It Wasn't Good For You

As You Suffered On The Cross

But You Were Not Afraid

Knowing Just What Sin Had Cost

God So Loved The World

And You Knew You Were The Plan

And For The Joy Set Before You

The Nails Went Through Your Hands

It Was Love That Put You There For Me

I Was The Joy Set Before You

And Now I Am Free

Because Of The Cross

And What You Did There For Me

It Was A Good, Good Friday For Me

Despised And Rejected

No One Seemed To Care

But I Know That I Was On Your Mind

While You Were Hanging There

I Will Ransom Them, You Said

From The Power Of The Grave

Pour Out My Spirit On The Earth

That All Who Believe Shall Be Saved

I'm Sorry It Had To Be This Way

But Lord, I'm Grateful

I Had The Chance To Say

Thank You, My Lord, My God And King

In You I Live And Breathe, I'm Born Again

With Those Nail Scarred Hands

You Rose Up From The Dead

Everything Had Come To Pass

Just As The Prophets Said

And You Ascended To Heaven

To Prepare A Place For Me

And My Soul Is Satisfied

Your Spirit Is With Me\\

IT'S A SPIRITUAL THING

You Know

I Don't Mean Half The Things

I Say To You

And Sometimes, You Know

The Other Half Just Ain't True

But There's One Thing

You Can Always Know

And I Know You Do

'Cause It's Written On My Heart, Lord

I Love You

Now, Lord, You Know

These Old Habits Of Mine

Are Hard To Break

And Sometimes I Think

That When I Finally Change

It'll Be Too Late

But Deep Inside

I Know That It's Comin'

And I Know It's True

'Cause It's Written On My Heart, Lord

I Love You

I Found Out All My Sins

Have Been Forgiven

By Jesus, Who Took Them On The Cross

They Say He's Made A Place For Me

In Heaven

It's A Good, Good Thing

Not To Feel So Lost

I Found Out Jesus Loves Me

No Matter What

And No Matter What

I'll Give My Best To Him

A Love Like This Can Only Come

From Heaven

'Cause It Makes Me Feel Like

I've Been Born Again

Deeper Than My Emotions

Higher Than All My Thoughts

This Love I Have For You

Will Never Die

Deeper Than My Emotions

Higher Than All My Thoughts

This Love I Have For You

Is A Spiritual Thing\\

LOVE FINDS A WAY

Love Finds A Way

To Soften The Hardest Heart

Love Makes A Way

When Everything Falls Apart

Love Is Of God, And God Is Love

Love Never Fails, It Is Forever

This Is How We Know What Love Is

Jesus Christ Laid Down His Life For Us All

This Is How We Know

We Belong To The Truth

We Lay Down Our Lives For Each Other

We Set Our Hearts At Rest In His Presence

If Our Hearts Condemn Us Not

We Are Confident In Him, Love Finds A Way

Love Is Patient, Love Is Kind

Love Is Not Jealous,

And Remembers No Wrong

Love Rejoices In The Truth

Believes, And Endures All Things

Love Finds A Way\\

MERCY WAS WAITING THERE FOR ME

Jesus, When I Look At What You've Done

On The Cross At Calvary

It Makes Me Stop And Think

About How Hard It Was

And That You Did It All

You Did It All For Me

I Found Mercy At The Cross

I Didn't Know That I Was Lost

Until You Found Me In My Sin

And Set Me Free

I Found Grace At The Cross

And The Faith To Believe

I Found Mercy Was Waiting There For Me

Waiting There For Me

I Just Want To Praise You, Lord

For Who You Are

Because You Never, Never Gave Up On Me

I Just Want To Thank You, Lord

For Seeking Me Out

'Cause When I Turned To You

You Were Waiting There For Me

Jesus, When I Look

At Where You Brought Me From

And How You Changed Me

From The Sinner That I Was

I Fall Down On My Knees

And I Thank You, Lord

You're The Best Thing

That's Ever Happened To Me

I Found Mercy At The Cross

I Didn't Know That I Was Lost

Until You Found Me In My Sin

And Set Me Free

I Found Grace At The Cross

And The Faith To Believe

I Found Mercy Was Waiting There For Me

Waiting There For Me\\

OH, WHAT LOVE

God Reached Down And Captured Me

Oh, What Love, Oh, What Love

God Chose Not To Remember My Sins

Oh, What Love, Oh, What Love

He Took The Pain That Bore My Shame

The Book Of Life Still Bears My Name

Forgiven And Free From The Bonds Of Sin

Forgiven And Free, He Gave Me New Life

And I'm Born Again

Oh, What Love The Father Bestows

Upon All Who Believe

God So Loved The World

That He Gave His Only Son

Oh, What Love, Oh, What Love

I Believed And He Rescued Me

Oh, What Love, Oh, What Love\\

ONE THING

There Is Only One Thing I Desire, Lord

There Is Only One Thing

I Will Ever Ask Of You, Lord

To Be Right Here With You

What Better Place

Could I Ever Hope To Find

Than To Be Right Here With You

Where Your Love Endures For All Time

And You Stay With Me

And You Speak To Me

And You Hear My Prayer

And You Help Me See

You Are The Way

The Truth, And The Life

My Savior, My Lord, And My Friend

Imagine, If You Will

Jesus Hanging On The Cross

Imagine, If You Will, His Lifeless Body

Serves No Purpose Anymore

Imagine, If You Will

Jesus Stepping From The Tomb

Imagine, If You Will

Jesus Stepping Up To You

Speaking Words Of Truth

What More Would You Have Me Do

Child, What More Would You Have Me Do

There Is Only One Thing I Desire, Lord

There Is Only One Thing

I Will Ever Ask Of You, Lord

What Would You Have Me Do

Lord, What Would You Have Me Do

There Is Only One Thing

I Desire, Lord, . . . You\\

ORIGINAL GRACE

Adam Why Are You Hiding?

Lord I Am Ashamed

I've Never Felt Anything Like This

We Are Naked And Afraid

The Big Mistake We Made In Life

By Listening To The Wrong Advice

It Was Not My Fault, Nor Was It My Wife

The Devil Made Her Do It

But I Didn't Stop It

We've Been Deceived

And Now We Gotta Leave

It's Never Gonna Be The Same

We Had A Good Run, But Now, We're Done

And Everybody Knows Our Name

We Can't Go Back To Who We Were

So Glad He Made These Coats Of Fur

Sacrifices All Around

And Everybody Knows Our Name

Everybody Knows Our Shame

Everybody Knows Our Pain

I'm Sorry You Had To Leave

You Shouldn't Have Eaten

From That Tree

Don't Worry, Though

I Have A Plan In Place

I'm Taking Away Your Sin

With Original Grace

I've Chosen To Send My Only Son

To Pay The Price

For What You've Done

He Will Give His Life

To Save The Human Race

This Is Original Grace

I Lift My Hands In Your Name

My Life Will Never Be The Same

By Your Power And Your Might

I Will Walk In The Light

Original Grace Has Saved My Place

Saved My Place In Heaven

Thank You Jesus

All My Sins Are Gone

All My Sins Have Been Forgiven

Original Grace Has Taken My Place

On The Cross At Calvary

And Now I Have A New Life All Because

All Because Of Original Grace

Lord I Give You All My Praise

Jesus, Name Above All Names

I Don't Deserve This Kind Of Love

This Love That Comes Down From Above

Jesus, My Lord, My God And King

Jesus, You Are My Everything

I Feel Your Presence In This Place

I Can See You On Each Face

I Feel Your Love

That Covers All My Sins

Crucified With Christ

I'm Born Again

Taking The Good News

From Place To Place

Signed, Sealed, Delivered

With Original Grace

Lord I Give You All My Praise

Jesus, Name Above All Names

I Don't Deserve This Kind Of Love

This Love That Comes Down From Above

I Feel Your Presence In This Place

Send Us Out With Original Grace

By Your Power And Your Might

I Will Walk In The Light

By Your Power And Your Might

I Will Walk In The Light

I Lift My Hands In Your Name

My Life Will Never Be The Same

By Your Power And Your Might

I Will Walk In The Light

With Original Grace\\

YOU MUST HAVE LOVED ME

The Day Came And Left

And I Finally Get It Now, I Understand

You Died Upon That Cross

To Take Away The Need To Judge Me

But Then You Rose Up With The Keys

To Death And The Grave

You Set The Captives Free

I Know You Must Have Loved Me

You Must Have Loved Me

To Deliver Me From The Dark

You Must Have Loved Me

To Want To Be My King

You Must Have Loved Me

To Shed Your Blood For Me

You Came And Found Me, Lord

You Must Have Loved Me

Now, The Days Come And Go

And Still, I Stand Amazed

At Your Saving Grace

Overcome By Forgiveness

That Never Fades Away

The Comforter Lives Within Me Now

Revealing This New Life

Lord, You Set Me Free.

I Know You Must Have Loved Me

You Must Have Loved Me

To Deliver Me From The Dark

You Must Have Loved Me

To Want To Be My King

You Must Have Loved Me

To Shed Your Blood For Me

You Came And Found Me

Lord, You Must Have Loved Me

Now, My Days Are Forever Filled

With Worshiping And Praise To Him

He Knows My Heart

And Hears My Every Prayer

My Lord, And My God

I Stand Before You Now

Lord, You Set Me Free

I Know You Must Have Loved Me\\

"God Will Always Do For You What Only He Can Do Through You"

BH

Made in the USA
Columbia, SC
01 April 2021